Easy Homeschooling

Curriculum

answers these questions and more:

- How do I reach our spiritual and educational goals?
- How do I make the most of the decade of impressibility" (ages 6-16)?
- How exactly does the literary method work and why is it effective?
- Should we read excerpts or entire books?
- What are the most important, and secondary subjects?
- How can I stimulate interest in a subject or topic?
- How do I teach so that learning becomes permanent?
- How does knowing and feeling contribute to will training?
- Why are these particular books best for these ages?
- How can nature study be combined with our reading topics?
- Is fantasy really appropriate for children, and if so, why?
- What is the best narration-notebook system?
- Where do I begin historical study?

Easy Homeschooling

Curriculum

by Lorraine Curry

www.easyhomeschooling.com

God's Gardener
Boelus NE 68820 USA

Easy Homeschooling Curriculum

Copyright © 2007 by Lorraine Curry
ISBN: 0-9709965-3-5

Book design and layout—Lorraine Curry
Editing—Lorraine Curry
Proofreading—Jean Hall

Chapter " Computers"
- The Holy Bible, *New International Version,* copyrighted © 1973, 1978, 1984 by International Bible Society
- Quotations from www.dictionary.com

"SpillMilk"— Ethan/www.fonthead.com

Dedicated to my Contributors

Mary E. Woodis
Maribel Hernandez
Christy Herbert
Kim Kautzer
Rachel Starr Thomson
JoJo Tabares
Robin Khoury
Penni Hill
Don McCabe
Leanne Beitel
Wendy Toy
Janice Campbell
Cyndi Kinney
Susie Glennan
Marilyn Rockett
Jean Hall

With Special Thanks to:

Jean Hall
Janice Campbell
Marilyn Rockett

for their continuing contributions to the Easy Homeschooing titles

Contents

~~~Part 2~~~

Foreword

When I read this book it spoke deeply to my heart's desire, both for me, and regarding my ideals for our children. Teaching our children to love God, and to live out that love through high morals and ideals, can be a hard thing. Mrs. Curry stresses two main subjects, history and nature study, through which we come to see the Lord's hand and His glory. I thought, "What a great way to teach them, through great literature." Still following and using her techniques, as outlined in her previous books, she guides the reader through rich literature selections that will challenge you and your children. In our culture of slang language and decadent amoral lifestyles, these selections are refreshing and challenging, reminding us that things were not always this way. The book is especially useful since there are many resources available to access the older books.

In *Easy Homeschooling Curriculum*, we are also privileged to hear thoughts of others on various important skill areas. These chapters offer helpful guidance in putting together literature-based studies. I am happy to see more than one chapter devoted to writing, as I think many are intimidated by this topic. There are also suggestions for spelling, vocabulary, speech, Bible, keyboarding and math.

After reading *Easy Homeschooling Techniques* and *Easy Homeschooling Companion* several times, I know that this book, also, will be a valuable and well-used resource: inspiring as well as challenging to all who read it.

—Christy Herbert, homeschooling mom to three children

Part 1

Introduction

Which subjects will best fulfill our goals as Christian homeschoolers? In this book, we will not only consider subject areas, we will also explore practical application of these subjects. First we will review the basics, such as our basic tools—*the Bible and literature*, as well as our basic technique—*reading*. We will then focus on the school subjects, which are the topic of this book. This book encompasses grade-specific techniques, suggested titles, topics of study as well as general method for history, geography and other important subjects.

What is really worth learning? In *Easy Homeschooling Curriculum,* we hope to give insight into that question, along with practical ideas for these most important subjects.

Herbert Spencer (1820—1903) was one of the most brilliant men of his generation. Although he is chiefly remembered as the father of Social Darwinism, his words give us food for thought about educational choices.

Men read books on this topic and attend lectures upon that, decide that their children shall be instructed in these branches and not in those: and all under the guidance of mere custom, or liking or prejudice, without ever considering the enormous importance of determining in some rational way what things are really worth learning.

Bible

Without a doubt, the Bible should have primary emphasis in our schools. We desire a moral result. However this result will not manifest overnight. This is why we should "be not weary in well-doing." The seeds of morality that we sow in our children take time to grow. Do not worry about the outcome, just keep sowing the seeds. Charles Alexander McMurry (1857-1929), American educator and author, said:

> There is much anxiety and painful uncertainty on the part of those who charge themselves with the moral training of children. Labor and birth pains are the antecedent to the delivery of a moral being.

The school years from six to sixteen are the formative years. That is when we must put forth our all-out best efforts. We choose to put aside many of our private interests for the sake of our children. We will never regret doing this, but we *will* have regrets if we do not. Along with packing all of the Scripture possible into this *decade of impressibility*, we choose to model Scripture in action by 1) our own example and 2) through the lives and deeds of men and women throughout history. Our concentration, then, should be on the classics.

Classics Defined

There are particular qualities that identify a classic book or poem.
- It communicates permanent and important truth.
- It transfers this truth to the reader in an artistic manner.

No matter when the work was written, to be considered a classic it will speak to our hearts today as much as it spoke to hearts of those long since gone from this earth. The human truths portrayed in classics are eternal, and make the work "eternal." Rather than fading, these truths shine with growing brightness, but only to those who continue to hold truth in this modern day.

Moreover, real literature has a creative touch. A good writer brings us into the story and setting, by words and phrases that play on our senses as well as our heart. Some works have such force, clarity and brilliance that we know only an artist could have created them. Such is the case with the polished gems of Thomas Gray's *Elegy*... and William Cullen Bryant's *Thanatopsis*.

Because the originator of a great work is its artist, we choose original works. In cases where the original work is in another language, we look to another creative master to translate. Some writers who have rewritten foreign language classics are Scott, Macaulay, Dickens, Kingsley (*Greek Heroes*), Hawthorne (*Wonder Book, Tanglewood Tales*) and Irving.

Purpose of Classics

The purpose of great literature is not to assimilate style, grammar or form, or even to appreciate literature as art—although all of these result from the use of literature. Rather, literature's ultimate purpose is morality—to produce God-fearing children and adults. When we turn our eyes toward this goal, education will have meaning and this goal will also motivate toward excellence in all subjects. Charles McMurray tells us:

> *Intense study of motives and conduct, as offered in litera-ture, is like a fresh spring from which well up healing wa-ters. The warmth and energy with which judgments are passed upon the deeds of children and adults is the original source of moral ideas. Literature is especially rich in oppor-tunities to register these convictions. It is not bare knowl-edge of right and wrong developed, but deep springs of feel-ing and emotion opened, which gush up into volitions and acts.*

The vast store of early literature is moral literature. With genuine literature, we are lifted into the presence of men and women who incite the moral nature. Through literature, convictions arise naturally. No contrived or enforced morals here. The child, rather, becomes one with the hero or heroine. In this identification process, enhanced by the vividness of story, moral judgments are formed in the child. The great advantage of this indirect teaching is that it is received by the child, whereas preaching—especially without supporting prayer—often falls on a deaf ear.

Throughout history, "greats" influenced future greats, as parents nourished their youth with great literature. We can continue following this "old path" by supplying abundant quality literature for our children.

> *Thus saith the LORD, Stand ye in the ways, and see, and ask for the old paths, where is the good way, and walk therein, and ye shall find rest for your souls. . .* (Jer. 6:16).

The emotions portrayed in great literature are *our* emotions, and literature's effectiveness comes about by the like-mindedness of those characters of literature and ourselves in this day. Right feeling and actions are strengthened by seeing these feelings and actions in others. Stories are effective because of their drama and interest. We see the characters' actions and then, moving on in the story, we see the results of the actions—good or bad. As interest in the character's life increases, the force of a false step or right act moves the hearer to make right choices in his or her life. Could it be that the widespread and increasing lack of character in our world today has been partly because of the lack of real literature in education?

> *Butter and honey shall he eat, that he may know to refuse the evil, and choose the good (Is. 7:15).*

With a strong foundation in the classics, your students will have an appreciation for what is beautiful and good and will come to reject poorly written, frivolous trash.

Practical Application

Ideally, literary masterpieces should be read in their entirety, not as excerpts in readers or other literature texts, although these have been used for years in public education. It is better if the entire work is read in a leisurely manner. Spending more time on one book results in greater interest and, consequently, greater permanent learning. Many times we do not appreciate a book until we have read several chapters. But then—suddenly—interest arises, the plot thickens, and we desire to read "just one more page" before putting the book aside. Even when we are away from it, the characters are on our minds. We become friends with the heroes. Great authors draw you into the book gradually. There is a great deal of preparation taking place before we become emotionally involved with the protagonist. This is good, because our identification with him or her is then more fully developed.

When we take our time with a book, the moral force of the masterpiece is that much greater. We see the big picture, not just a few individual actions of the characters. In great books, the characters face serious problems in life. Only by reading the complete work will we fully see the actions resulting in problems, and how the characters overcome these problems.

Reading entire books also gives us a meal from the authors, not just a fleeting taste. We feel their "heart," get their full meaning, and learn to judge their artistic merits—and apply those to our own writing and expression, a definite aim in using literature for education.

When you read shorter works such as poems, additional poems and works related to the original should be read.

- Ideally, these will be poems or books by the same author and about the subject or time period.
- Read works about the same period by other authors.
- Least desirable for a unified historical study, is to read poems and works by the same author, about different subjects or times. See more below under "History" about combining works for your historical studies.

Note: See Bible teaching and literary technique explained more fully in *Easy Homeschooling Techniques* and *Easy Homeschooling Companion*. Also see ideas for teaching the Bible later in this book.

The Starring Subjects

After Bible, the most important subjects are as follows:

- History
- Natural History—science, particularly nature study
- Formal Studies—math, language, drawing, etc.

History best cultivates morality, **natural history** reveals the external created world in all its beauty, variety and law—and thereby the Creator—while the *formal studies* enhance and train in the ability to express the two other primary realms of knowledge. The formal studies can be begun as part of the thought studies (Bible, literature, history, etc.) as the student completes reports and undertakes research. Later the formal studies can be perfected as a tool for further expression of the thought studies. In practical terms, this means that you start reading aloud with your child from interesting books, beginning in the earliest years. All the while, your child is assimilating learning from the "formal" areas, especially composition, spelling, vocabulary and grammar. Later your older child will study the formal fields more fully to improve these very important areas of education.

1
History

After Bible, history is the most important school subject. Ancient cultures nourished their youth on the traditions of their ancestors. How much more important for us today to impart the character of the great men and women of history to our children!

History, a study of men, is also a study of morals. Each story, each action, demands a moral judgment. *Did he do right? Was that the wrong decision? What were the consequences of that action?* We desire to know the heart-qualities of the individual. History's chief purpose is to teach morals by example, not to pump facts and figures into the child. The teacher, too, will benefit and be made a more worthy example of character by these readings of high-quality histories, biographies and works of historical fiction. Here parent and child bond forever in common quest of high character. The teacher's delights become the child's delights. Carefully choose your interests in all areas, knowing that your child will surely follow.

Goethe said, "The best is good enough for children." Charlotte Mason recommends, not sketchy stories, but complete life-pictures of men and women and their surroundings. In order to have the best moral effect, use literary historical works throughout the grades. In this book, you will find grade-specific subject techniques, along with suggested works. High-quality materials are selected for each year while the subordinate subjects flow from this central nucleus of history.

American History

Not every period in every country's history is worthy of study. American history is rich with moral heroes. American schools should focus primarily on American and English history. For Early American history, use descriptive writing such as that of Bancroft and Irving, "Landing of the Pilgrim Fathers" by Felicia Dorothea Hemans, Webster's and Everett's orations, *Evangeline, Hiawatha,* Indian legends and life, *Miles Standish, The Knickerbocker History* and other original papers and letters. Then incorporate other countries' histories as they relate to American history. When studying the American Revolution, you could also study other revolutions such as the French Revolution. Other works that relate to this American period are the stories of Siegfried (Germany), Alaric (Italy) and Ulysses (Greece).

Start with earliest American history (and Bible history) with both the young child and the beginning homeschooler, no matter what elementary grade level they are. Begin your studies with the settlements. Everything had to be built from nothing. Thus early America is a good place to start. The child will be able to logically relate and comprehend when you begin at this beginning.

Principle Epochs of American History

- Ocean Navigators—Columbus, Drake, Magellan and the explorers— Smith, Champlain, LaSalle, Fremont and others
- Settlement and the French-Indian War
- Revolution and Articles of Confederation
- Constitution and Self-Government
- Civil War Period
- Industrialization
- World Wars
- Twentieth Century to Current Events

Some of the people to study in American history are Winthrop, Penn, Oglethorpe, Stuyvesant and Washington in early American history; DeSoto, LaSalle, Boone, Lincoln, Robertson in the Mississippi Valley; and in the West, Lewis and Clark; and current figures such as Ronald

Reagan, Condolezza Rice and President George W. Bush. True leaders are morally strong and superior. Our children's moral natures are formed by hearing of them and approving them. Biographies of these men and women:

- arouse strong interest
- implant moral ideas
- exemplify a period of history

These stories made our present good life possible. By reading of them, you honor the memory of these people with thankfulness to God. In honoring them we identify with, and "fix" our place as honorable citizens in this day and age.

A classic often gives us a picture of an entire age in an engaging manner. For instance, Scott's *Marmion*, in portraying feudal Scotland, also give us a look at feudal Europe. It unlocks the doors to ideas and forces of historical importance. To enhance this study, read *Ivanhoe*, the Crusades, Roland, *Don Quixote, The Golden Legend* and *Macbeth*.

For the United States' Civil War period, I highly recommend *Uncle Tom's Cabin* and Whittier's poems. Read Lincoln's speeches. Search out other great men and women of the time. But remember, in all of your reading, the choice is yours whether to read or not to read a work.

Choose the best biographies of people such as Charlemagne and Cromwell. Choose novels such as *Hypatia, Ivanhoe, Last Days of Pompeii, Romola, Uarda* and *Robinson Crusoe*. Read the heroic Greek myths. Read about Siegfried, King Arthur, Bayard, Tell, Bruce and Alfred. Such stories have the power to transform youthful minds because they are interesting and exemplify good motives and actions.

Suggested Works

- *Little Lord Fauntleroy* by Frances Hodgson Burnett
- *Life of Martin Luther* by Julius Kostlin
- *Autobiography by Benjamin Franklin*
- *Adam Bede, Ramola* by George Eliot
- *Evangeline* by Henry Wadsworth Longfellow
- *The Lady of the Lake* by Sir Walter Scott
- *Julius Caesar* by Shakespeare
- *Uncle Tom's Cabin* by Harriet Beecher Stowe
- *Aenid* by Virgil
- *Divine Comedy* by Dante
- *Idyls of the King* by Alfred Lord Tennyson
- *Miles Standish* by Longfellow
- *Anabasis* by Xenophon
- *Punic Wars* by Livy
- *Lives* by Plutarch
- *Gallic Wars* by Caesar
- *The French Revolution* by Thomas Carlyle
- *Life of Washington, Life of Columbus* by Washington Irving
- *Iliad* and *Odyssey* by Homer

People to Read About

- John Winthrop
- William Penn
- Roger Williams
- James Oglethorpe
- Sir Walter Raleigh
- Christopher Columbus
- Samuel Adams
- William Tell
- David Livingstone
- Abraham Lincoln
- Robert Fulton
- Bible Patriarchs

History's Supporting Cast

- Oral Language and Composition
- Geography
- Drawing
- Science

Oral Language and Composition

After each day's reading, the students either tell back (narrate), or write summaries of what was covered. Details about oral language and composition are covered in my books, *Easy Homeschooling Techniques* and *Easy Homeschooling Companion* and also in Cindy Rushton's writings. ***www.cindyrushton.com***

Geography

The study of geography should cover the same region as the history study, not unrelated places near and far. For early American History, study North America and the Atlantic Ocean, including rivers, bays, forests and mountains.

Later, with the Westward movement, study the Mississippi Valley, a most striking feature of American geography with its lakes, highway rivers and streams. Study the forests that housed game, concealed enemies, had to be cut down. There is much detail as well as an entire picture in each geographical area, all related to each period of history.

Note: See more about geography later in this book.

Drawing, The Arts

Drawing supports history and geography.
- Maps can be drawn of the area studied.
- Do nature sketches of the indigenous flora and fauna.
- Listen to music from the period studied.
- Study and reproduce the art of the period you are studying.

Leave no stone unturned in this supplemental learning. However, remember that your primary aim is moral character, and your primary tool—after the Bible—is historical study through literature.

Note: See basic drawing instructions in *Easy Homeschooling Techniques*.

Science

Science can flow from Geography. After studying an oceanic area, study ocean life. Every epoch of history has related scientific topics. Be sensitive to them and undertake further research. When studying the History of the Westward movement study the forest animals such as the beaver—what an intricate example of God's handiwork, perfectly adapted for his work. Study topics 1) related to your studies and 2) those you or your children have an interest in. Natural history topics are endless. No one will ever be able to study them all. Remember, you are seeking deep knowledge of few things, not superficial knowledge of many things.

> *O LORD, how manifold are thy works! in wisdom hast thou made them all: the earth is full of thy riches* (Ps. 104:24).

2
Interest & Apperception

I nterest keeps the mind alert and active, leading to a steady accumulation of knowledge. *Apperception* is the process that takes place in the mind, when new knowledge is based on familiar knowledge; when we relate new ideas to familiar ideas. Both interest and apperception are are natural aids in the learning process.

Interest will motivate the child, even to accomplish difficult tasks. We are concerned here with genuine or direct interest—not the indirect interest that comes from rewards, or competition, that can generate selfishness and self-centeredness. Direct interest pushes the student to conquer difficulties, and gives a permanent pleasure in the studies. It is essential to develop interest while the child is young. Reading aloud on varied subjects is a proper tool for this, along with nature study. In addition, do not neglect to show interest in the child's interests. This also greatly develops a child's intellect.

Sources of Interest

In learning, the sources of interest are many and varied. One is stirred by the variety and novelty of things seen, another is concerned with the whys of the matter, and yet another is awakened by what is beautiful and grand in nature and art. Stronger yet is the interest that flows from common humanity. This is the reason that biographies and novels are important in education. There is also the social aspect, the concern regarding the good of nations. Last, but definitely not least, is religious interest—knowing that God is sovereign and good, and that we truly make a difference in His plan.

Specific Interest to General Knowledge

A sunflower in all its glory is a specific specimen, that when studied, leads to the general knowledge that flowers have Latin names, parts with names and so on. From sketching and then labeling the sunflower drawing, the individual parts are learned. The Latin name may be looked up. The habitat of the sunflower becomes known. Then you can go on and compare other flowers to your specific sunflower study, examining how the others are alike or different. Knowledge is increasingly acquired—general knowledge of flowers and even knowledge about plants in general.

A nearby mountain, its history, geology and weather can lead to a study of mountain ranges in general. In *Easy Homeschooling Techniques,* the example is given of traveling to Arizona, visiting a desert museum and then studying deserts in general, through reading and other projects.

In history, the study of a single character or characters moves to the study of the period, culture and geography. Individuals shine and draw out interest that later expands to greater knowledge. You could also study Bible characters such as David, Abraham, Moses, Esther, Hannah and Paul and then go on to missionaries, cultures and countries.

A first taste of any subject should always be the brightest, most beautiful and meaningful specimen, individual, poem, artwork or book.

A

First

Taste

Permanent Interest

The interest that we should strive to awaken in our children should be permanent interest. When your children are young, keep the learning boundaries open. There is time enough to develop individual gifted-ness and leanings. However, do not let a variety of interests lead to superficial knowledge. Too many "subjects" can easily cause this. Instead, especially for young children, keep to the primary subjects of history and nature study—bringing in the others as they arise natu-rally. Drawing and English can easily become part of nature study, whereas geography can be studied along with history. Let there be a natural flow, and not the "brain-switch bell" that divides one class from another. Instead of focusing on quantity of learning, focus on quality and depth of the current topic. Study it all day, all week, all month or even longer if that is where the interest lies.

Cramming facts into children is futile. You are wasting your time, because most facts, for most people, will not be remembered. The truth is, facts are usually not valuable except for the rare individual who is a contestant on a game show. What you want to develop, instead, is a genuine desire for learning and knowledge. With this as your quest, facts will be remembered, especially those that interest your child. Al-though your children will never learn everything about a subject, they will have the tools for further study if they so desire.

The Will

The qualities of the mind are knowing, feeling and willing. The will needs to be the controlling force, for strong character resides in the will. A primary purpose of learning is to build a strong will, inclined toward good and against wrong. Until built, both learning (knowing) and feeling will help in this construction job. As the child learns from godly examples in great literature, sympathies come into play and the will is strengthened. Some of these feelings are desire to please, ambi-tion, love of knowledge and appreciation of the beautiful and good. Other, more negative, emotions arise such as hatred for evil. The study of great literature thus strengthens the will. As the child approaches adulthood (high school), he or she needs to be stimulated to look at the subject from opposing angles, even to critique it to verify truth or exceptions. In this way, the child becomes a thinking person ready to set out in life, pursuing his or her goals with success. In truth, education's goal is will-training. We seek the result of a will that is guided by moral ideas. No preaching will be as effective as the influence of present and past lives lived well.

Concentrated Knowledge

A small amount of well-articulated knowledge is more valuable than a large amount of loose and fragmentary information. (McMurry)

Learning is more effective when associations are made in the learners' brains. To create associations, take time to research the geography, history and other ideas read about. If you read about a palm tree, there is no better time to study tropical geography, and even history. To teach in this manner, you must be flexible, not rigid. Never forget that you have many years to reach the goal of having well-educated children. Do not worry about covering an era, or a wide scope of history such as American history, in only one year. Take enough time on each period to accumulate collected and concentrated knowledge. No other learning will be permanent. A spattering of facts has no permanent hook in the brain. However, concentration strengthens confidence and character.

In 1895, McMurry prophesied:

> *The most striking feature of our public schools now is their shallow and superficial work . . . . the disease will grow worse before a remedy can be applied. . . . children were not born to be simply stuffed with knowledge.*

Joseph Payne in *Lectures on the Science and Art of Education* succinctly says, "Learn something thoroughly and refer everything else to it."

Refer your supporting subjects to your primary subject. Always double effectiveness, and save time, by basing your language lessons (writing, etc.) on your historical or nature lessons. Do the same with drawing.

In order to most effectively discover a subject, request that your children tell you what they want to know. Write each point down. You are not finished with this subject and topic until all questions are answered, even those that will come up in researching the present questions.

Double

your

Results

History and science are interconnected. When studying Bible history and other early history, the most logical science to study is natural science. When studying a later period in history, study the inventions and scientific discoveries of that age. There is a natural process of acquiring new ideas through ideas already learned. This makes learning much easier and quicker. This process is called *apperception*.

Apperception

It is very important for us, as Christian homeschoolers, to make sure that a strong Biblical and moral foundation is laid. As new ideas enter the picture, the old ideas are adjusted and yet, most often, the student goes back most strongly to the original ideas. McMurry in *General Method* says:

> *Oftentimes, therefore, older ideas or thought masses, being clear, strong and well digested, receive a new impression to modify and appropriate it. This is especially true where opinions have been carefully formed after thought and deliberation. . . . Sometimes, however, a new theory, which strikes the mind with great clearness and vigor, is able to make a powerful assault upon previous opinions and perhaps modify or overturn them. This is more apt to be the case if one's pre-*

vious ideas have been weak and undecided. In the interaction between the old and new the latter then become the apperceiving forces. Upon the untrained or poorly equipped mind a strong argument has a more decisive effect than it may justly deserve. As we noticed above, new ideas, especially those coming directly through the senses, are often more vivid and attractive than similar old ones. For this reason they usually occupy greater attention and prominence at first than later, when the old ideas have begun to revive and reassert themselves. Old ideas usually have the advantage over the new in being better organized, more closely connected in series and groups; and having been often repeated, they acquire a certain permanent ascendancy in the thoughts. In this interaction between similar notions, old and new, the differences at first arrest attention, then gradually sink into the background, while the stronger points of resemblance begin to monopolize the thought and bind the notions into a unity.

Process

Apperception happens automatically. Although in the beginning the baby understands nothing, his or her knowledge store is built, "line upon line." This knowledge store becomes so vast, eventually, that thinking of a person or hearing a train whistle draws from the storehouse details on not only that person but their interests, books read, studies and so on; and of that train, such things as trips taken, vistas viewed and traveling companions. Later, new knowledge builds upon old and we are sometimes surprised by new conclusions upon considering new ideas.

Likewise, with literary learning, when you continue on with a subject, but from a new angle, such as another author's view of it, interest is sure to be present and strengthened.

Importance

Since all future knowledge is based on present knowledge, it is important that we make current learning permanent. This is why the daily oral or written narration is so important. As the student rethinks the topic at hand and reiterates it in the summary, it become permanent knowledge to him.

Because of this, it is also very important that we choose that which is worth remembering. We must build constantly, on this store of knowledge, a stronger and stronger foundation for future studies. Familiar ideas should not be neglected but repeated. Repetition here does not mean review, or repetition of books, but of ideas, each new title building upon the character built by the last great book. Indeed all fields of knowledge are based on apperception—acquiring new knowledge based on old. In math, a child would not master long division if the times tables were not known. In creating realistic art, color would be of no use, if skill in execution were not first acquired. And in nature study, deeper things of science are learned from familiar things. Therefore, in all learning we carefully make sure the foundation, then build upon it, stone by stone.

Make

Learning

Permanent

3
Nature Study

History looks at the past to reveal the best moral examples, while nature study opens the door to the present real world in all its beauty, variety and law. While reading, spelling, language and arithmetic are tools for acquiring and formulating knowledge, history and nature study are knowledge in themselves. They are the "thought studies" whereas subjects such as reading and writing are "form studies." In reading aloud and early nature study, thought studies precede form studies, as they should.

Friedrich Adolph Wilhelm Diesterweg, nineteenth-century German educator said:

> *No one can afford to neglect a knowledge of nature who desires to get a comprehension of the world, and of God . . . or who desires to find his proper relation to Him and to real things.*

A purpose of natural science study, now usually known as "nature study," is to acquire the ability to observe and discern, to discriminate and compare objects, in investigation or experimentation. One of the most important needs of educated man is that he retain his inquisitiveness—his awe at God's world—and nature study trains in this vital trait.

Aims of Nature Study

- Entertainment through animal stories that also teach facts and morals.
- Utility—*What plants are beneficial? Which harmful?*
- Training of the senses.
- Development of the intellect (accurate thinking) by analyzing and classifying the specimens.

Yet there is a higher goal. We should seek out insight into nature to better appreciate Creator God. Through nature, God meets our needs and shows His love for us. Although twenty-first century man rarely notices, the birds still sing for us, showing God's love to all who will see. "He doeth all things well." Nature reveals His character, which is well-ordered, productive, unchanging and efficient (which should also be our character). Thus we have nature study as the subject second in importance to history in our primary goal of building moral character.

The Simple Approach

If nature study is systematic from first through eighth grades, much science will be learned. Therefore, elevate nature study to a regular subject with its own time slot. Study life and habits, homes and organs

of insects, plants and animals. Study a squirrel to see how it was perfectly created to live in its surroundings. Discover how the squirrel relates to the nut tree and how the weather affects the tree. All work together, mutually beneficial, as the Designer so perfectly planned. While man separates the sciences, in creation all are interdependent—weather, rocks, seasons, plants, animals, and so on. Nature study will result in accurate thinking, self-reliance, inductive thinking and respect for the Creator.

Winter Nature Studies

By Mary E. Woodis

Bad weather doesn't have to ruin the most wonderful nature walk ever! Just dress your darlings according to the weather and go outside any- way. It will be fun to quickly gather a few interesting finds or better yet, take the time to look around. There are many things that can be learned by going outside when the weather turns nasty.

- *Have you ever wondered where the birds go when it rains?*
- *What about the ants?*
- *If the wind picks up, is it blowing in the tree tops or only along the ground?*
- *In what areas are the puddles forming first?*
- *Which way is the runoff headed and why?*
- *If it is cold outside, how are the animals protecting themselves from the cold?*
- *What are the birds doing to survive?*
- *Why is it their delicate little feet don't freeze?*
- *What about the plants?*
- *How are they reacting to the cold?*
- *Are there plants that are still green? How is that possible?*

Now you have plenty of fuel for a wonderful nature study. Fix your- selves some warm drinks and cuddle up. Get your favorite nature guide or just surf the Internet together for an enjoyable time of discovery. Nature study doesn't have to end just because the weather isn't coop- erating. If the weather or your health absolutely prohibits even a quick trip outdoors, take the time to check around inside and see what you can find. Every house has a few bugs, plants or both!

Discovery Indoors

Go ahead and give your children the freedom to look in all of those out-of-the-way places and find those bugs. Go before them and make a list of what you find, and make it like a treasure hunt. Look at houseplant communities—tiny flies, mites, spiders, earwigs, aphids, ants, ladybugs or ladybird beetles; silverfish, millipedes, termites in dark places. Give them tweezers or some other bug catching picker-uppers, a bug container to put them in, and let them go. When they come back with their finds, get out the sketchbooks and let them draw that bug's portrait! Let them use a magnifying glass to really look closely at these critters. God has created these, "creeping things that creepeth upon the earth," in such infinite detail, it would be a shame not to use this opportunity to marvel at His creation. It was the sixth day of creation when God created these things, and now we need to take the proper time to praise Him for His provision on this rainy (or snowy) day. Teaching your children to look more closely, and include all the details in their sketches, will train them in the habit of observation and open a whole new world to them. This also helps to teach them the power of attention. These habits will serve them their whole life.

What to Do with Your Nature Find

- Identify your find—use field guides, the Internet or encyclopedias.
- Sketch your find—be sure you provide your budding artists with the best art supplies.
- Photograph your find if you have reluctant artists. Sometimes it is more fun to just take a picture.
- Display your find attractively.

Are your little artists done with their sketches yet? Be sure that you (or they) have written the Latin name and the common name at the bottom. Don't forget the date and the artist's name. Over the years, if you have more than one child, that priceless piece of art might become anonymous. We have cut our sketches out with scrapbooking scissors and stuck them on decorative paper. Then, on another sheet of paper my children copied a poem or Bible verse. After that, I turned them loose with my scrapbooking supplies and came back later to some beautiful creations. In this fashion we have built attractive nature notebooks.

Displaying Nature Finds

In the beginning we had a designated table, shelf or general area to display our nature finds. We have used the ledge of the living room windows, the top of the TV and—sometimes—the biggest shelf on the china hutch. Over time, we had so many treasures that they became part of our home decor. Here are some ideas to use your finds.

- Scatter fall leaves around a candle on a mirror for a centerpiece.
- Light a dark corner in the winter by twining lights around budding branches.
- Pile your rocks in a dish over a small pump and add water to create a waterfall.
- Use acorns and dried okra pods to create Christmas tree ornaments.
- Press spring flowers, glue to a background and frame to make a lasting piece of artwork or even a personal greeting card.
- Use sea shells, snail shells or discarded egg shells from birds or turtles and rocks from a stream bed around a candle.
- Have a special table for your nature finds.

The scarf or tablecloth on your special table should reflect your theme or the current season. Anything can go on this table. Your children will really enjoy this simple creation once they catch on to the idea. My children have brought me interesting shaped stones, birds' feathers, nuts, pine cones, branches, leaves, an abandoned turtle shell, discarded birds' eggs in the spring, miniature pumpkins in the fall and a bouquet of flowers that could be dried. You get the idea!

Mary Woodis is the wife of Jessie and the mother of three blessings: Jessica, Emily and Parker-Daniil. We can be reached at 1365 County Road 74, Florence, AL 35633 or on the Internet at jessiew@hiwaay.net We offer many articles and resources to help you on your journey.

www.crookedpinespublishing.com

Showcase Your Nature Finds

By Maribel Hernandez

In your nature studies, you will want to showcase your children's finds. Why showcase your students' work? Because they need to be recognized by their parents. This increases confidence in their abilities, while providing a learning opportunity.

In addition, this is a great excuse to explore plants. Grow your own medicinal plants or pick from the many existing plants, such as dandelions, already blooming on front lawns or in backyards during spring time. Even if you cannot identify the botanical name, collect it anyway. You can always do that at a later time. Take pictures of the plant before you pluck it. Be sure to take lots of pictures of all views, top, side and bottom.

Use a flower press to dry your collection. I press my plants in an oak flower press Pete made for me, however you can purchase these at craft stores, or check the library or the Internet.

Here are some ideas for displaying your finds:
- **Library Display:** Nearly every library has display cases. Some libraries work around themes, like summer, spring, fall and winter, while others are very flexible. Contact your local librarian for details.
- **Science Fair:** After you display your student's plant collection at your local library you can showcase it at the next science fair.
- **Websites:** Many homeschool support groups have now gone on-line. If your support group does not have a student page, you can suggest it to them. Here is a perfect place for you to upload your student's botany work. If your homeschool support group website does not have enough space for pictures you can always get a free account at *www.photobucket.com.* They allow you to upload pictures free of charge to any site you choose.
- **Blogs:** A blog is an on-line journal. Blogs are a combination of two words, web and log. You can post digital pictures of your plant collection, along with details about the plants and your nature outings.

- **Journals:** Your journal could be a three-ring binder, a composition notebook or any other writing journal.
- **Home Herbarium:** After you are all done showcasing in all the above areas, you are ready to retire your student's plant collection to your home herbarium. A herbarium is a collection of plant specimen archives, displayed with a detailed record of the flora of that particular area. Many universities that teach botany have one on campus. Your walls are a perfect place to showcase your student's plant collection. Use your home herbarium to archive and record your student's work in botany. You can preserve your collection un-mounted or mounted.

Note: Before you showcase your student's work in botany, explore which plants you would like to showcase by reading what plants have been used for, what they could be used for and finally, what your student will use plants for. Here are some of the things your children might come up with, when asked the following questions:

What is Made from Plants?
- clothing from cotton
- medicine-aspirin from willow
- rope from flax
- spices such as cinnamon
- houses from logs
- toys from balsa wood
- tables from mahogany
- chairs from cherry
- furniture from pine
- fences from wood
- power line poles from wood
- warming a house by burning logs
- teas from dried raspberry leaves

What could you make from plants?

- children's paint from crushed blueberries
- tea by boiling fresh mint leaves
- air spray freshener by mixing water and spearmint oil in bottle sprayer
- rope work by tying knots using flax fibers
- breakfast by boiling oats and adding strawberry jam
- snack by mixing dried fruit & nuts
- toy by building a sail boat from a balsa kit

Make a chart for your children and make a copy for each child. Title it, "What will you make from plants?" Then have columns headings of "What?" and "Plant." You might also wish to have a column for further notes.

4
Intro to Early Grades

The earliest educational activity is oral work, particularly 1) reading aloud to the child and 2) having the child tell back to the adult. If you are able to begin this when your child is very young, you are blessed indeed. There are untold advantages to beginning these methods early. We must not limit our great God, but some say that if a child has not been given a taste of, and acquired a taste for, age-appropriate great literature by the age of ten, he may never do so. Without this concentrated technique, your child could become scatterbrained instead of learning the habit of undivided mental attention. Our tools are the Bible and great books, and our basic techniques are reading, reading aloud and narration. Our most important subjects are History and Nature Study. Interesting books stimulate interest, while knowledge is built upon knowledge. Now we will begin to look at specific techniques for the subjects, and at books by grade level.

With the preschooler, repetition of favorite character-building stories and poems is not harmful. The child will be thoroughly familiar with the story and soon perhaps even recite back a rhyme, word for word. The story and the lesson will be a permanent fixture of the mind, laying the foundation for true culture as well as character.

Do not wait to introduce literature until the child can read (see *Easy Homeschooling Techniques* to find out how to teach your child to read). At about age ten, or before, children will be able to read stories for their own enjoyment, but from age four or earlier they can receive an abundance of mental stimuli and instruction through being read to, listening to books on tape and being told stories and educational facts. Such a mind becomes productive, inquisitive and receptive to the printed word when it begins to acquire knowledge through individual reading.

The suggestions herein can be tossed together and combined for all of your children in these approximate grade levels. Works that are read aloud in the earlier grades, can be reread, topics researched and reported on in the later grades. However, specific grade-level suggestions will be made in this title. Read the entire book to get the big picture and then go back and plan your ideal curriculum based on your children's ages. See planning details in *Easy Homeschooling Techniques,* and actual diary entries from our own school in *Easy Homeschooling Companion.*

Classic literature for this age group includes nursery rhymes, folklore, fairy tales, fables, the classic myths and *Robinson Crusoe.* Some of the best selections for rhymes come from Shakespeare, Ruskin and Kingsley. Young children, being naturally joyful, can relate to rhymes more than any other age. The musical language is remembered and quoted for years. Fairy tales appeal to this age group, for this genre speaks to the young child's soul.

Is fantasy appropriate for Christians? Children are closest to heaven, with their innocence and creativity. They are made by God with an aura of fantasia. There is spontaneity and vivid imagination. We do not hesitate to allow fiction for older children and adults, why then should we disallow it for those who are that much closer in their natures to it? The child lives in *this* world, whereas adults only see it in relation to their storehouse of experiences. However, I believe that even in our adult lives we should maintain a touch of this dreaminess, this awe. Indeed, if we did, our lives would continue be more alive and joyful, as the child's naturally is.

We are led to reality through fantasy. Although fictional, these stories model real standards, real character, real personality. Children naturally put life and personality into inanimate playthings. Reality and fantasy are intertwined. When children see a real bridge and village, they might build one from their imagination in the sand; they read a fairy tale, then act it out in the here and now. While some will stand numb and helpless when faced with barriers, the child whose imagination is allowed to run free at this age will have more real problem-solving ability and confidence as an adult.

Should we then quench this vivid imagination and deny such literary feeding? Although we differentiate between Bible truth and fantasy, we allow our children to enjoy the story-making artistry of early literature. Our resources would be quite meager if we did not.

History, although our most important subject, is not introduced as a subject until grade four, when its concepts are more readily grasped. The exceptions are short historical studies related to holidays such as Thanksgiving. See more details regarding history, see the chapter, "Grade Four."

For all grade levels—for the Christian homeschooler—the Bible is preeminent. Bible resources for the early grades are the *King James Bible,* especially for memory work, and Bible story books such as *Hurlbut's Story of the Bible.* Bible teaching was covered extensively in my books, *Easy Homeschooling Techniques* and *Easy Homeschooling Companion.*

5
Preschool, Grade One

Fairy Tales, Fables, Classic Myths for Children

Children are enthralled with fantasy and this natural inclination will only open their minds to be educated through creative literature as they mature. Fairy tales are the early seeds that produce creativity and freedom of expression. Fairy tales are not primarily for enjoyment. We have both the moral goal and the creativity model. The door to the child's heart is imagination, and this literature brings the child into the story so that the story can then do its work. The story carries its own moral. The bad of the story teaches as much as the good. The child—in independently judging the actions portrayed—grows in morality and intelligence. Therefore, stories with a stated moral are not as good for training in morality. Some of the best stories for this age are *Grimm's Fairy Tales*.

> *There runs through these poetic fairy talks the same deep vein of purity by reason of which children seem to us so wonderful and blessed.* —Jacob Grimm

The babe—in his pure essence—is nearest to God, to the heavenly kingdom, so is it any wonder that he lives in this world? He can relate well to royal living, and take on princes and princesses for playmates.

In addition, after the Bible, no other literature can prepare the child for later artistic comprehension, enjoyment and skill. Where did greats such as Shakespeare get their poetic inspiration? We can well guess that he, as well as so many others, were nutured on not only the Bible, but on legends and fairy stories. Charles Kingsley said this world is:

> *marvellous and fantastic... a most pure part of their spiritual nature, a part of the heaven which lies about us in our infancy, angel-wings with which the free child leaps the prison-walls of sense and custom and the drudgery of earthly life.*

In your teaching, there is no need to emphasize the moral element in any way. The inherent moral nature of the child will take note of it. Your child's intelligence is capable of—and will be further developed by—its own thought processes. To preach may only insult this intelligence, thereby creating barriers to moral learning. J. Klaiber said:

> *When we look into the trusting eyes of a child, in which none of the world's deceit is to be read as yet, when we see how these eyes brighten and gleam at a beautiful fairy tale, as if they were looking out into a great, wide, beautiful wonderworld, then we feel something of the deep connection of the fairy story with the childish soul. . . . the fairy tale and the child's soul mutually understand each other. It is as if they had been together from the very beginning and had grown up together. As a rule the child only deals with that part of real life which concerns itself and children of its age. Whatever lies beyond this is distant, strange, unintelligible. Under the leading of the fairy tale, however, it permits itself to be borne over hill and valley, over land and sea, through sun and moon and stars, even to the end of the world, and everything is so near, so familiar, so close to its reach, as if they had been everywhere before, just as if obscure pictures within had all at once become wonderfully distinct. And the fairies*

all, and the king's sons and the other distinguished person-
age, whom it learns to know through the fairy tale—they are
as natural and intelligible as if the child had moved its life
long in the highest circles, and had had
princes and princesses for its daily play-
mates. In a word, the world of the fairy
tale is the child's world, for it is the world
of fancy.

The fairy story clearly portrays good and evil.
While evil may triumph for a time, in the end
good prevails. All the virtues are portrayed. Biblical principles are immediately identified by
those with prior Biblical knowledge. (Yes, read
the Bible and Bible stories from this earliest
age.) Faithfulness is admiringly portrayed in such passages as this from
Jacob Grimm:

> Lenchen: "Leave me not and I will never leave thee."
> Fundevogel: "Now and nevermore."

In the good fairy tales, disobedience and dishonesty are strongly pun-
ished. A definite Christian thread runs deep through these tales. The
first becomes the last, love is shown for the downtrodden and burdens
are lifted.

Although fairy stories break the rule of reading whole books, the
themes are interconnected and unity will be achieved. The child will
make the necessary connections for lasting value.

Fairy Tales for Preschool, Grade One
- Grimm's Fairy Tales
- German Fairy Tales
- Grimm's German Household Tales
- Stories from Hans Christian Andersen

Fables

Fables are stories in which the main characters are usually animals with human characteristics and include a moral, or lesson. They are appropriate for this age group because children have a tenderness toward animals. Fables often portray troubling relationships that can be objectively judged by the children. Particularly in Aesop's fables, character traits are highlighted and results made plain. Greediness or selfishness is quickly compensated. This lays the foundation for future moral training. This teaching is simple and to-the-point, not merely lofty ideas or virtue for their own sake. Fables teach Gal. 6:7 "...whatsoever a man soweth, that shall he also reap" in the clearest manner. The parent can merely mention a fable to remind the child when tempted toward a particular fault.

> *The peculiar value of the fables is that they are instantaneous photographs which reproduce, as it were, in a single flash of light, some one aspect of human nature, and which, excluding eveything else, permit the attention to be entirely fixed on that one.* —Felix Adler

Like the myths, fables are quoted much in literature and a background in them will help with future literary understanding and enjoyment. Moreover, such stories will be moral reminders to your children even after they become adults.

Fables for Preschool, Grade One
- *Aesop's Fables*
- *Book of Legends, Book of Fables and Folk Stories* by Horace E. Scudder
- *The Book of Nature Myths* by Florence Holbrook

Other Works

- Bible Story Books
- Mother Goose
- Classic Myths
- *A Child's Garden of Verses* by Robert Louis Stevenson
- Children's Poems

Practical knowledge can come from fairy tales and fables, for they touch on reality in some ways—kings, chickens, foxes, marriage, farmers, houses, fields and so on. Questions will come up and these things can be researched or talked about. The child who makes a friend of an animal through a fairy tale, will not mistreat a pet. This tenderness will also carry over into care for other weaker or smaller beings.

Ask for narrations from this youngest group—allow them to tell back the story in their own words while you transcribe in a notebook. Here you will see what impressed that particular child the most. Do not be concerned if the moral vein was not noted by the child. It may have been noted, although not reported, being overshadowed by other things, or it may be that in a future story, the moral message will be more fully realized. When it does—when it comes from your child's heart alone—your heart will smile.

Buy big notebooks for each child, add each child's narrations consecutively in his or her notebook, with the book or story title at the top of each narration with the complete date, so that this treasure book can be enjoyed for many, many years, even potentially by his or her descendents. When one notebook is finished, number and date it and go on to a new one.

Interesting stories will accelerate the child's desire to master reading for himself. Perhaps your young child is able to write. Then, composing and spelling can also be brought into these studies. (See *Easy Homeschooling Techniques* for detailed how-to's for these subjects and others such as drawing.) Pursue "artistic narration" as the child draws what he or she has "seen" in the story. You could add a drawing course at this age. Make sure it is one that teaches how to draw realistically.

Fairy tales create a fine entry into nature study. A new interest emerges in the plants and animals of the story. This age group loves to see and describe rocks, plants and pictures and do number work based on objects. Children are drawn by specific people or things, not general principles. Let them see an actual palm tree not just read about palm trees.

In the first and second grades, simple number concepts can be learned from number of lobes of leaves, petals on flowers, etc. Basic math—addition and subtraction—may be taught. Later, trips can ignite studies of miles, distance and various topics such as depth of rivers, oceans and height of mountains.

Grade One Course of Study

Suggested activities assume an arithmetic course, starting at whatever grade you desire. The child has many years to learn the basic math concepts. However, these basics should be learned very well.

- **Reading**—Stories from good literature, as suggested herein, presented orally and reproduced by the children. Beyond the suggested books, you could begin reading interesting biographies.
- **Nature Study**—Observe flower, plants, insects and animals. Also see books by Karen Andreola, Cindy Rushton and Karen Skidmore Rackliffe.
- **Drawing**—Illustrate the stories you have read. Study realistic drawings. Sketch flowers, animals, birds.
- **Writing**—Compose short sentences, or even just select words.
- **Picture Talk**—The child describes appropriate illustrations and artwork.
- **Copywork**—As able. The child copies verses from the Bible or excerpts from the works being read.
- **Grammar**—Basic grammar corrections based on writing done by the child.

6
Grade Two

Robinson Crusoe, Hiawatha

Robinson Crusoe by Daniel Defoe is the first "whole book" introduced to the child, the fairy tales and fables being individual stories. This more realistic story, in its most original form is the primary selecton for this age. One old original was published by Houghton,
Mifflin & Co. in the Riverside Literature Series. *Robinson Crusoe* is a
multi-faceted learning tool, teaching many things from practical skills
to problem solving abilities. Whereas with the fairy stories, "anything"
was possible, now the child will be faced with—and deal with—the limi-
tations of reality. Crusoe is an ordinary man, who has to face and solve
problems with his limited knowledge. He not only faces and resolves
problems, he philosophizes about them, which also gets your child's
brain "working."

Rousseau also chose this title as the first educational volume for
the main character of his book, *Emile*. (See *Easy Homeschooling Companion*, "Harvesting from History.") He thought that Emile should
learn from this title the "delight and glory of irresponsible natural life."
However, Robinson Crusoe is a highly moral book. Crusoe's morality
springs from his experiences and is eventually shown by his concern
for his fellow-man. His longing for home and loved ones is an intense
theme of the book. Although a thoughtless youth, eventually his
thoughts turn to important matters. He finds a Bible, and it does its
unfailing work on him. He recognizes what brought him to his fate.

Diligence is one charteristic of morality. In Robinson Crusoe, children are brought face to face with the principle and importance of hard work. The child begins to realize and appreciate the effort needed to meet even his or her basic needs. Crusoe is taxed physically—and mentally—and has to deal with failure. Your child will identify with Crusoe and grow in maturity, self-reliance and creativity. He or she will begin to know the complex systems of the world in the simplest manner—a good place to start. Daniel Defoe is a literary master and makes us feel as if we are living Crusoe's experiences. Children take the story into their playtime, building caves and copying the protagonist's lifestyle in other ways. Other learning activities are varied:

- *Narration*—The best and easiest "next thing" after reading aloud, is to have the child narrate. You may also question about—or discuss—particular parts of the reading.
- *Field Trips*—Visit sites that relate to the story. Consider zoos, artistic potters, other trades and occupations and history museums.
- *Rustic Crafts*—Make baskets, mold clay to make vessels, even make rustic furniture. Let the story give you inspiration.

Teach
Accurate
Observation

- *Geography*—For the first time geography comes up—continents, Europe, islands, coasts, bays, rivers, hills, mountains, seas and so on. Climate may now be introduced as the island climate is far different from what Crusoe had left behind.
- *Science*—Many plants and animals are introduced. However, it is best to study those that the child is most familiar with. This could include tropical fruit, parrots, goats and pigs, as well as other birds, fish, fruits and grains.
- *Drama*—Scenes between Friday and Crusoe may be acted out. Appropriate costumes and settings may be utilized.

- *Drawing*—Teach accurate observation for drawing skills (see *Easy Homeschooling Techniques*). Animals, plants and other subjects may be drawn by the children.
- *Independent Reading*—The child, if able, reads the book, or an adaptation (choose carefully, an older edition is usually much, much better), and undertakes projects and reports based on his or her own interests.

For an etext of this title, as well as of other classic books, see Bibliomania.com. Their summary of the book follows.

www.bibliomania.com

Daniel Defoe's most famous novel was published in 1719 with the full title, The Life and strange and surprising Adventures of Robinson Crusoe. *It is based, in fact, upon the experiences of Alexander Selkirk who had run away to sea in 1704 and requested to be left on an uninhabited island to be rescued five years later. Defoe himself was in his late fifties when he wrote the book, which is often considered to be the first English novel. Crusoe ends up on a desert island in the manner of Selkirk. With only a few supplies from the ship he builds a house, a boat and a new life. His island is not wholly uninhabited, though, and there is the exciting but ominous presence of cannibals who Crusoe occasionally encounters and saves a native from. The latter becomes his servant, Man Friday. The crew of a mutinying ship finally rescue our hero, but it is his adventure on the island that interests us. The story has remained popular ever since its publication and it spawned two sequels: later in 1719 with* The Farther Adventures of Robinson Crusoe *and a third part,* The Serious Reflections of Robinson Crusoe, *in 1720 which consisted of moral essays. The first novel, though, is particularly notable for its detailed verisimilitude allowing us to believe in the situation—something assisted by the uncomplicated language used by the author.*

Hiawatha

A literature professor told me that good books begin at the beginning. The Bible is our model, while "Hiawatha" also begins at this logical place:

> *By the shores of Glitche Gumee, . . .*
> *Beat the shining Big-Sea-Water*
> *There the wrinkled old Nokomis*
> *Nursed the little Hiawatha,*
> *Rocked him in his linden cradle,*
> *Bedded soft in moss and rushes . . .*

Children learn about the richness of nature from *Hiawatha*. Nature is central with thoughts, activities and even man himself being one with it. Indeed Hiawatha has warm communication and friendship with the animals and trees of his forest home. This will draw the child's interest into nature appreciation and study. In the gathering of the tribes from all over, even from "the far-off Rocky Mountains," we have openings for geographical study. Search for the places mentioned and find them on a map, then sketch a map. The children can draw tents, bows and arrows, pine forests and all other things mentioned. You can visit museums. Before reading the poem, you could read a commentary and give the children an introduction.

Hiawatha Prayed & fasted

Morality is clearly revealed. Hiawatha prayed and fasted, not for himself, but for the good of his people. Consider lines such as this about Hiawatha's honesty with friends Chibiabos and Kwasind:

> *Long they lived in peace together,*
> *Spake with naked hearts together . . .*

Home life is described through the fairy tales within the poem. From childhood to manhood we see descriptions of family customs such as weddings, parties, games and even work—a happy view of life to be admired and emulated. This poem also promotes love and compassion for mankind, yes, even for those who may seem to be our enemies in this very day.

> *Listen to the song of Hiawatha!*
> *Ye whose hearts are fresh and simple,*
> *Who have faith in God and Nature,*
> *Who believe, that in all ages*
> *Every human heart is human,*
> *That in even savage bosoms*
> *There are longings, yearnings, strivings*
> *For the good they comprehend not,*
> *That the feeble hands and helpless,*
> *Groping blindly in the darkness,*
> *Touch God's right hand in that darkness,*
> *And are lifted up and strengthened . . .*

Such musical lines make memorization and recitation a delight. Choose favorite passages and commit them to memory. See "How to Memorize" in *Easy Homeschooling Techniques,* Chapter 6, "Combining Subjects." However, do not be surprised if some of the passages are memorized automatically by the children, particularly those that are repeated in the poem. This is the "Mother Goose" of classic literature.

Grade Two Course of Study

- **Math, Reading and Reporting**—Continue as in Grade One Course of Study, but read and report on the books for this grade.
- **Nature Study**
- **Copywork**—Copy selected passages from the suggested works.
- **Vocabulary**—Look up unknown words from the works read and have your child copy into a vocabulary notebook.
- **Write**—Children may write short original sentences, if able.

- ***Spelling and Grammar***—May be taught as they arise in the child's writing.

7
Grade Three

Classic Myths, Bible Stories, Robin Hood

I n the third grade the focus is on simple and appropriate classical myths. Such myths have been rewritten for children by Nathaniel Hawthorne (*Wonder Book* and *Twice Told Tales*) and Charles Kingsley (*Greek Heroes*). Kingsley said to the children:

> *For nations begin at first by being children like you, though they are made up of grown men. They are children at first like you—men and women with children's hearts; frank, and affectionate, and full of trust, and teachable, loving to see and learn all the wonder around them; and greedy also, too often, and passionate and silly, as children are.*

Avoid complex myths at this age, such as "Tales of Troy." Choose rather "The Golden Touch," "Perseus," "The Chimaera" and the "Golden Fleece." The myths take the child into the bright and clear heavens. His soul soars with a magical quality that will remain with him, and will keep his life from the downward pull of the dull and ordinary. Although both deep and lofty, the stories are simple, not complex. We are introduced to heroes, whose ambition, chivalry and generosity are rewarded—heroes who meet danger or other personal challenges head-on, for the sake of a higher purpose.

Because America does not really have a mythical age, we also lay claim to, as indeed we can, the myths of Europe. American writers also refer to the spirit and the characters in these myths. Our Christian heritage is much greater. We have similar stories; however, ours are true.

The Bible Stories

It goes without mention that the Old Testament stories (and indeed the entire Bible) are best of all for children. The Old Testament stories have been taught internationally no matter what creed. There is a universal standard of morality, and this standard comes to all of us through God and His Word. Although other religions may have adapted, changed, eliminated and neglected some of it, the basic foundational truths of morality remain. Simple yet God-like characteristics shine through Bible characters, making the Bible the best morality-building tool. Even if seen only as literature by some, the Bible contributes to high character. Bible stories are also a good introduction to select English poems such as "Burial of Moses" and Milton's "Samson Agonistes."

This would be an ideal time to begin presenting art history. Study the renderings of Bible stories by great artists. Talk about them. Write about these paintings, and even—should you desire—reproduce them or small parts of them. One method of copying artwork is to draw a grid on a copy of the original and a grid on the paper or canvas, then reproduce each small section. Bringing the focus in like this helps tremendously in accurate drawing.

Robin Hood

Howard Pyle in his preface to *The Merry Adventures of Robin Hood* tells the reader that even though the childhood of Robin Hood seemed to be carefree, it was basic training for maturity. He learned to take hard knocks, manage anger and endure discomfort without revealing it. Robin Hood and his men swore never to hurt a child nor harm a woman in any way. This is all presented to the child in an entertaining manner, even humorous at times. Skill prevails over brute strength. One of Robin Hood's most impressive qualities is his sharpness and adaptibilty based on the immediate circumstances. Although the government considered him an outlaw, he is known as a champion of the people. Because of this duality, *Robin Hood* will provide fuel for the fire of discussion. In justice remember mercy—we must remember the times in our judging, for feudalism itself showed injustice to the downtrodden and poor. From this desire for human rights sprang the great issues of liberty for the common man. The stories give a picture of feudal English activities as well as English character. They give background information for such other works as Sir Walter Scott's writings, Kingsley's *Hereward the Wake*, Jane Andrew's *Gilbert the Page* and Tennyson's *"The Foresters."*

Robin Hood's band loved the forest, the song of the bird and the fragrance of wildflowers. These nature pictures draw the hearers into a deeper interest in and appreciation of nature. In addition, the language used is a melodius example of English.

> *All the air was laden with the bitter fragrance of the May,*
> *and all the bosky shades of the woodlands beyond rang with*
> *the sweet song of birds,—the throstle-cock, the cuckoo, and*
> *the wood-pigeon,—and with the song of birds mingled the*
> *cool sound of the gurgling brook that leaped out of the forest*
> *shades, and ran fretting amid its rough gray stones across*
> *the sunlit open glade before the trysting-tree.*

Selections for Grade Three

- *The Merry Adventures of Robin Hood* by Howard Pyle
- *Some Adventures of Robin Hood* (less complete edition) by Pyle
- *"The Foresters"* by Alfred Lord Tennyson
- *Ivanhoe* by Sir Walter Scott

- *Greek Heroes* by Charles Kingsley
- *"Jason's Quest"* by James Russell Lowell
- *Adventures of Ulysses* by Charles Lamb
- *The Story of Siegfried* by James Baldwin
- *The Age of Fable* by Thomas Bulfinch
- *Iliad, Odyssey* by William Cullen Bryant
- The Bible Stories
- Greek and Norse Legends
- Ballads and Legendary Stories
- Ulysses, Jason, Siegfried

Jean Hall suggests:
- *The Children's Homer* by Padraic Colum
- *Men of Iron* by Howard Pyle
- *The Little Duke* by Charlotte Mary Yonge

Grade Three Course of Study

In grade three you may also read stories about Washington. Read local history including stories about Native Americans and their customs, and immigrants. Study geography of the locality—hills, streams, valleys and so on. Some of this could be covered around Thanksgiving.

Same as previous grades, along with:

- Writing short papers
- Spelling and grammar related to the child's writing
- Writing familiar poems from memory

8
Creating Books

By Christy Herbert

In our homeschool, for the first three grades, we are going to focus on history and nature study, according to Lorraine's suggestions, but I want to include creating books. As they get used to the older-style literature, they can dictate to me their own stories, which they then can illustrate. My children really enjoy this process of creating. They also enjoy listening to the stories we read, and then trying their hand at recreating them. As to filling in with specific titles, I am using many of Lorraine's suggestions. Many of my books are going to come from Yesterday's Classics book site, as the owner shares with me future titles that she is going to print. I like to hold the book in my hand, instead of reading an etext off the computer.

In grades one through three children can have a hard time putting pencil to paper to express their thoughts. This can be a great time to use narration and dictation. Narration lets them tell you about stories or anything else. Dictation is when you write down what they say. A child who can narrate or dictate what he or she read, or was read to him, is a child who *knows*.

Narration is nothing new. Charlotte Mason, an educator from the late 1800's said, "They can narrate what they know." Narration is the telling back. Making my children narrate their instructions back to me helps both them and me know that the instructions are clear. However, I use narration primarily after I have read to them. Narration is deceptively simple and yet complex. When they are telling back, they need to mentally run back over what was just read. It needs to be in sequence, and they need to make judgments about the piece. My children, many times, will add in phrases and vocabulary from the piece read. This is an important reason to use quality literature. Children will pick up many ideas and notions from literature—that is why we want it to be moral.

I like to help my children express themselves more fully with their narrations by the use of dictation. As they narrate, I write down what they have told me, and then sometimes they will illustrate their narrations.

These techniques can lead to some exciting original stories. It gets very exciting and animated when they dictate original stories to me. All the previous tales that they have heard are now available as models for their stories. You can see the wheels of imagination begin to turn, as their minds work to solve problems in the stories they tell, as plots and characters begin to develop.

Many skills now come into play. Along with problem solving and character development, they will learn to not fear or dread writing. They will also have a sense of accomplishment and pride in seeing their written words, and learn that their thoughts are important enough to be recorded. One more thing I learned is that as they learn to read for themselves, you can use their own narrations as readers. As it is their story, they should be quite familiar with it.

Wheels of
Imagination
Turn

If you are wondering what actual writing your students will be doing, I recommend penmanship and copywork for grades one through three. We will also include phonics and math in our curriculum.

These ideas are not original to me but a combination of those of Charlotte Mason and Valerie Bendt. Mrs. Bendt has a lovely book and DVD called *Creating Books with Children* which shows how to make actual books. You can find these at:

www.ValerieBendt.com

9
Grade Four

American History: Discoveries and Explorers

In grade four the child begins historical studies. The European tales of the first three grades are not really historical, however they give a taste and introduction of what is to come. The earliest American history continues in this heroic vein. No other country has had such a beginning. While early European history begins in myth or savage warfare, our own is about ideals and principles. In the myths and previous stories, characters stood against fictional dangers, but now individuals stand tall and strong to overcome very real, sometimes extreme difficulty. There is no better history for the purpose of teaching morality than American history. American history tells of the making of an American. It took the European, in his fine dress, from the carriage into the canoe, from being served to being self-sufficient. Little by little he conquers America, and America conquers him. Americans will begin with America and end with America, introducing European or world history as it corresponds to similar events in America. Those from other countries can carry on a similar course of study with their country being central.

Start with local or state history. This is preferable because the resources are plentiful, while concepts of basic settlement are simple and universal to all areas. The dangers and difficulties were similar for pioneers and nation builders everwhere. Because of this, we make an exception to chronological study. The chronology to young children is not the important thing, but rather that they are strongly impressed by the leading characters and events of early American history, beginning with their local history. Keep it simple. Focus on explorers and early settlement—the beginnings. More complex historical periods, such as wars, are best left for later grades.

Biographies are best , simplifying history. We want to provide the children a rich feast of the highest character and ideals. Search out the best books about your state. Nebraska has Willa Cather, Mari Sandoz and others. My favorite Nebraska living history book, *History and Stories of Nebraska,* by Addison Erwin Sheldon, relates interesting incidents from pioneer life. Accounts by Native Americans will also add color to your state study. New Yorkers could start with Hudson and Champlain, while Virginians could study Raleigh and Smith.

Bring in foreign study as it applies to American History. Use books as Lanier's *Boy's King Arthur,* Frost's *King Arthur and His Court* and other stories about King Arthur, and also parts of Spenser's *Faerie Queene.* Other options are *American Life and Adventure* by Edward Eggleston, *The Arabian Nights* or *Child Life in Prose and Verse* by John Greenleaf Whittier. You could read about:

- Abraham
- Joseph
- David
- Moses
- Romulus: and the founding of Rome
- Plutarch's Coriolanus
- Cincinnatus
- Caesar's conquests in Gaul and England
- The Angle's and Saxon's invasion of England
- Alfred's war with Danes, labors for his people

Remember to spend enough time on these stories so your child has more than short, scrappy information. Bring in detail, pictures and maps. Visit historical sites and living history museums. We natually look for Past's picture at the location of the event. The thoughts, feelings, motivation, activities and hardships endured will all become more real when the spirit of locality is realized in conjunction with histori-cal studies.

Needless to say, literature is also one with history. The Bible, for instance, strikingly combines history with poetic delivery. Poetry truly paints realistic pictures of the past. Some literary gems to use with history are:

- "Lays of Ancient Rome" by Macaulay
- "Illiad"
- "Odyssey"
- The story of Siegfried
- Arthurian legends
- "Marmion"
- "The Lady of the Lake"
- "Courtship of Miles Standish"
- "Evangeline"
- *Julius Caesar*
- *Henry VIII*

Orations such as those of:

- Daniel Webster
- Edmund Burke
- Cicero
- Demosthenes

Historical novels such as:

- *The Talisman* by Sir Walter Scott
- *The Virginians* by Thomas Babbinton MacCaulay
- *The Spy* by James Fenimore Cooper

Even essays such as those by:

- Macaulay
- Carlyle
- Motley
- Emerson
- Lowell
- Schurz ("Essay on Lincoln")

Other books, ballads, poems and stories:
- *Grandfather's Chair* by Nathaniel Hawthorne
- *Tales of a Grandfather* by Sir Walter Scott
- *Biographical Stories* by Nathaniel Hawthorne
- *Tales of Shakespeare* (some) by Charles Lamb
- *Lives* by Plutarch
- "Rip Van Winkle"
- "Sleepy Hollow"
- "Dolph Heiliger"
- "Great Stone Face"
- "Hiawatha"
- "Sheridan's Ride"
- "The Oregon Trail"
- *Autobiography* by Benjamin Franklin
- "Songs of Labor" by John Greenleaf Whittier
- "Cobbler Keezar's Vision"
- "The Merrimack"
- "Mabel Martin"
- "Snowbound"
- "Horatius at the Bridge"
- "Paul Revere's Ride"
- "Barbara Frietchie"
- "The Battle of Ivry"
- "Battle of Blenheim" by Robert Southey
- "Grandmother's Story of Bunker Hill" by Oliver Wendall Holmes
- "Alexander the Great" by Plutarch

Grade Four Course of Study

In grade four your child will begin historical studies with local history. He or she will also continue with writing, narration, copywork and other suggested activities for earlier grades. For a more complete Course of Study, see *Easy Homeschooling Techniques*.

10
Intro to Later Grades

History is our most important subject and this section will provide suggestions for grades five through eight, based on the early American model of education, where the child was considered educated by the eighth year, and the most important topics were covered before eighth-grade graduation. However time has added more history, and there is always more to learn, so in high school the student can study additional and more complex history, including current events, as well as other subjects such as advanced math, speech and other electives.

Children from grades five through eight are interested in the adventures and excitement of history, not the philosophy and details of government. The beginnings of America are simple and easily comprehended by this age group. However the books selected are not necessarily simple to comprehend. You will see why your children's video usage should be greatly limited or preferably totally eliminated—and much reading aloud done—from an early age, when you see what titles they should be comprehending at these ages. Sure, they may become more educated than we are. That's the point! But do not fret if they do not seem to be getting the complex ideas. Present the works as a buffet and let your child take what they will. Do not revert to dead history, dates and facts only, with the life squeezed out!

History is comparisons resulting in recognition of contrasts and similarities. During some years, older methods of transportation will be contrasted with those of the period being studied. People groups will be compared, as will battles, wars, financial situations, inventions, territories and even statesmen. Your children will contrast the idea of strong central power (Franklin, John Adams, Hamilton, Washington, Webster, Lincoln) with the idea for stronger states' rights (Samuel Adams, Patrick Henry, Jefferson, Calhoun and Jefferson Davis). Some review of topics previously covered will bring in these comparisons as the new topics are studied. This process aids in producing adults with independent-thinking skills. Comparisons need not be forced, but used when current study and past knowledge bring comparison naturally to light. However, when used, comparisons foster stable independent thought.

A good composition assignment that can be reused without tedium, is to have your child compare a current topic or person with one that he or she has previously studied.

History is problems, and problems solved. Problems become more complex, the closer we get to the present. Examining problems and contemplating solutions also helps develop a fair-minded thinking "man." When studying the American Civil War, for instance, be sure to look at both sides.

Although the framing of the Constitution is studied in grade seven, the Constitution has been a major thread running through all American history. Each decade provides its own tests of the Constitution's strength and flexibility in meeting the demands of a growing country. One could even say that the history of the United States consists of illustrations of the meaning and intent of the Constitution.

> # History is Problems Solved

What should the child learn in history study? He or she should learn the most important dates and facts, the work of men, the growth of institutions, the rise and fall of nations, tyranny, as well as patriotism and self-sacrifice. A by-product of history study will be morality and maturity as the student begins to make rational judgments on historical events.

Many titles are suggested in *Easy Homeschooling Curriculum*. Look for older copies or reprints of these titles at:

www.hstreasures.com

www.yesterdaysclassics.com

www.mainlesson.com

www.easyhomeschooling.com

www.addall.com/used

www.oldfashionededucation.com

www.gutenberg.org

11
Grade Five

I n grade four, discoverers and explorers were studied. This included Lewis and Clark, David, King Alfred, Tell, Bruce, Wallace, Greek and Roman stories, Siegfried, Roland, Hannibal and Caesar; while Hudson, Magellan, John Smith, Raleigh, and others, created interest in their European countries.

Both fourth and fifth grades deal with early American history, namely the explorers and very earliest settlers. Similar European stories supplement and enhance. This period is from approximately 1492 to 1850. Although chronology is not too important at this point, a few dates can be noted and simple timelines drawn (see *Easy Homeschooling Techniques*). The important thing is that the dramatic focused stories of individuals be told, keeping interest high and eventually uniting to form the big picture.

Geography should be a part of history study. Fourth, fifth and sixth grades will cover North America and the United States, but also European geography as it arises in the reading. (See more on geography later in this book.) Fifth graders will study:

- *European Explorers*—Columbus, The Cabots, Magellan, Cortes, DeSoto, Coronado, Drake.
- *American Explorers*—George Rogers Clark, Lewis and Clark (journey up the Missouri), Fremont (two expeditions in the Rockies, California and 1849 gold rush) and Powell.

- **European History**—Isabella of Spain (Christians and Moors in Spain, conquest of Granada). See Washington Irving's stories about these topics.
- **Prince Henry and DeGama**—Exploration of the coast of Africa. How the Portuguese tried to find an eastern route to India, compared with Columbus' and Spain's efforts westward.
- **English History**—William the Conqueror, Conquest of England, Richard I (his crusades and knightly adventures), John and the Great Charter, Elizabeth in connection with Raleigh and Drake, The Armada. Books: *The Story of the English* by Guerber, and *Child's History of England* by Dickens.
- **Scottish History**—William Wallace and Robert Bruce. *Tales of a Grandfather* by Scott.

The following supplementary titles can be used as necessary or for the child's independent reading:

- **American**—*Hiawatha* by Longfellow, *American Explorers* by Higginson, *Heroes of the Middle West* by Catherwood, *Discovery of the Old Northwest* by Baldwin, *Colonial Children* by Hart, *Source Book of American History* by Hart, *American Historical Tales* by Morris, *Children's Life of Abraham Lincoln* by Putnam.
- **English and Scottish**—*Tales of Chivalry, Tales from English History* and *Tales from Scottish History* by Rolfe. English and Scottish heroic ballads. *Robin Hood* by Pyle and *Story of the English* (early parts) by Guerber.

Other European Stories

- *Lays of Ancient Rome* by Macaulay
- *"Jason's Quest"* by Lowell
- *Ten Boys on the Road from Long Ago*
- Stories from *Herodotus*
- *Story of the Greeks* by Guerber
- *Story of Roland* by Baldwin

- *"Ulysses among the Phaeacians"* by Bryant
- *Odyssey of Homer* by Palmer
- *Book of Golden Deeds* by Charlotte Yonge

Most of the above are, or include, famous stories that should be known by children. Even though time in class may be limited, children have untold hours to devote to this pleasurable and yet important learning activity. This is so much better than TV, videos and computer usage!

Geography

Geographical studies for this grade focus understandably on North America, which then becomes a *type* for future studies of other continents.

Other Fifth Grade Titles

- *Black Beauty* by Anna Sewell
- *King of the Golden River* by John Ruskin

Fifth Grade Course of Study

- ***Writing***—Summaries, letters, checks, reports, dictionary use.
- ***Grammar and Spelling***—Based on writing. Also spelling of states, capitals and geographical features. Formal simple grammar may be taught. Mastery of a few basic concepts is important—capitalization rules and basic punctuation.
- ***Other Subjects***—Continue with math and nature study-science. Add anything else you like.

12
Geography

Geography is an integral part of your historical studies. Without it your child will not completely understand, nor remember, history. Historical decisions were made upon geographical factors: mountain ranges established boundries of countries; hills and seas influenced locations of cities; rivers determined trade routes; and military operations were hindered or helped by geographical conditions.

View pictures of the places studied, put up wall maps and use the globe. Use black or whiteboard outline maps, or let your child draw and label their own maps. Map-making and coloring was one of my favorite school activities. Use Prismacolor® pencils for the best results.

The quantity of topics in geography, as well as in every subject, is practically infinite; therefore, we need to choose carefully a few of the most important topics to study in depth. This is far better than gaining merely surface knowledge in many things. Choose limited precise "type" studies and spend more time on each. Select particular topics such as a city, a river, or a lake. Study, for instance, a nearby mountain range in depth. Knowledge of all mountain ranges will be ingrained by this one focus. This study will keep interest high because the topic is real and "touchable."

One thing will lead to another from geology to spirituality. Pursue these paths, while whetting the child's appetite for more. Time is limited, but knowledge is not. Even if time dictates we go on to another subject, the child will—as interest leads—pursue further knowledge of advanced concepts (such as chemistry, geology and physics) either now or in the future, and most probably, independently. Always encourage this curiosity and research.

Remember the rule, "from home outward." However, choose a greater nearby geographical feature over an insignificant, but even nearer one. Although we have wall maps and a globe readily available, and the child may have a limited knowledge of the big picture, more real knowledge—especially for younger ages—will be gained by bringing the focus in on the detail. Later these concepts will be applied to lands and geographical features both far and near. These features will bring the reading, locating, map studies and map drawing together into an exciting whole.

Many books have been written on teaching techniques; however, in the grain of Easy Homeschooling and my personal view, even geography can be best and most easily covered by reading and mandatory reporting by child. The retelling is what makes the knowledge permanent. I would add some picture viewing or even videos for enrichment and further understanding. Tests here are okay, such as map labeling. Children should know certain facts, such as states, perhaps counties, capitals and primary geographical features, and eventually oceans and countries—at least the primary countries.

13
Grade Six

This year the primary topic will be European History in addition to the colonial history of America—the early settlement and the growth of the colonies and the French and Indian wars up to the Revolution. We begin chronological study of the development of the colonies—the early progress of America.

I was asked if the selections in this book were indeed suitable for these age groups, and not too difficult. Although some things, at first mention, *seem* complex, such as this year's study of charters, taxation and religious disputes, life in early American was actually simple.

In the fourth and fifth grade, biographies were the major tool for historical study, and in the sixth grade they are also prominent. A notable example is Franklin's *Autobiography*. When studied in the biographical format, bigger issues are clarified. People are inherently interesting, and to use that interest in teaching our children is of great value. Our main characters for this grade are William Penn, Benjamin Franklin, Miles Standish, John Winthrop, Roger Williams and others. This grade builds the foundation for deeper study in the next year's investigation of the causes of the Revolution.

Other worthy topics are customs, family life, religion, the plan of government, and the French and Indian War. These will be seen in the books recommended below.

Spend plenty of time on the uniqueness of each of the four major colonies. Experience the lives of the colonists, the dangers, the hopes, the dreams and the faith. A focus on a few rich episodes of this period will give greater lasting knowledge than a survey (such as found in text books) that attempts to cover everything that happened.

In examining the settlers of each of the colonies, we begin to be drawn across the Atlantic to both Europe and Africa. At this period the "melting" had not begun in the "pot" of America, and cultural distinctions can be clearly seen. By studying these interesting differences, our children today will see how then—as now—out of many peoples we became one nation. In early times, the richness of diversity was striking and notable, while today we often get mere glimpses, such as—in this locality—on one weekend a year, "Polish Days," with authentic old-country music and dancing. Allow your children to get bright pictures of each culture of the colonies, which will lead to interest in the countries the settlers came from.

Source Material

Source materials, including autobiographies, are excellent, along with biographies. The best biographies are written by authors who lived at the same time as—perhaps even knowing—the person written about. Read this touching passage from *The Life of Washington*, Vol. IV, by Washington Irving. A woman told of seeing, as a child, the British leaving and Americans returning worn and forlorn at the end of the Revolutionary War.

> *We had been accustomed for a long time to military display in all the finish and finery of garrison life; the troops just leaving us were as if equipped for show, and with their scarlet uniforms and burnished arms, made a brilliant display; the troops that marched in, on the contrary, were ill-clad and weather-beaten, and made a forlorn appearance; but then they were our troops, and as I looked at them, and thought upon all they had done and suffered for us, my heart and my eyes were full, and I admired and gloried in them the more, because they were weather-beaten and forlorn.*

These eyewitness accounts are unparalleled in their power to make the past come alive. Hart's four volumes (see below), for instance, touch every important period in our history. No text book or even single author could add such richness to your historical study. Hart says:

> *The source . . . throws an inner light upon events, secondary writers may go over them, collate them, compare them, sometimes supplement them, but can never supersede them.*

Savor

the

Source

Source material develops the thinking process in a greater way than commentaries of any sort. With source material the child must make judgments, since that has not been done for them. With the truth, instead of opinion, the child is free to make accurate assessments. The brain is quite capable, and in fact "desires" to be used in this way.

Chronology

This grade looks at the small beginnings of the colonies, onward to the greater organization and strength that came with growth— from town meetings to representative government. It shows the essence of self-government from its simplest origins. Studying the four or five leading colonies and comparing them reveals this self-reliance in more detail. They were similar and yet different. Similarities included wilderness location, problems with natives and self-defense. They were different in labor, religion, local government and social character, along with cultural diversity as already mentioned. When each colony is compared, the review enhances permanent knowledge. (See the chapter on review, later in this book.)

The colonist themselves eventually had to compare and reconcile their differences to unite into one nation. When you study the colonies and this period of history in this depth, you will not have to return to this period, but will be able to go on to other epochs and other nations in future years. Later topics will build on this foundation, such as, in what ways this period of government became the model for Constitutional government. Even slavery was an issue that began in this early period. These connections will produce a thinking child, and future adult, in a way that learning mere dates and events could never do. Children are quite capable of reasoning when they are provided with enough material. These works will provide just that: fact, eyewitness accounts, illustration, biography, adventure, and examples of everyday life. The study of these earliest settlements, and the domineering forces of Europe that caused the colonists to begin to unite, are the stepping stones to the information studied in the seventh grade. The most dramatic event of this period (sixth grade study) is the struggle for control of North America between the French and the English-Americans. The intimate relationship between the Americans and the Europeans lead into a study of relative topics in Europe. We study these to see "their side of the story," the background to the conflicts of this period, as well as those of the future. Other factors that come to light are reasons for emigration, religious persecutions, and inherent desire for the freedoms that America offered then, as now. The study of Colonial America is thus a study of the systems and people of England, Holland, Sweden, France, Scotland and Ireland as well as Africa.

Geography's focus this year is on Europe as well. Use maps and globes to find the places you read about. Pictures, prints and other historical items can be viewed. Visit historical museums.

European History

- *Persian Wars*—contact of Persia with Greece
- *Darius and Xerxes*—Marathon and Plataea
- *The battle of Salamis* and the leading characters
- *The Punic wars*—Rome vs. Carthage, Hannibal and Fabius, Regulus
- *The Scipios*—the courage of the Romans

Colonial History of America

- *Virginia*—James I, Bacon, Washington. Early government. Royal governors. English foundations. Colonial life in Virginia.
- *New York*—Stuyvesant and the Dutch. Royal governors. Native Americans.
- *Pennsylvania*—Penn, Franklin, Quakers, Germans, Scotch-Irish. The people. Early government, and plans for unity of colonies.
- *Massachusetts*—Plymouth and Boston. Winthrop. Representative system of government. Indian wars. Royal governors, charters and assemblies. Religious controversy and persecution.

European Conflicts Related to America

- Last French and Indian war
- Braddock's expedition
- English and French conflict
- Pitt in England
- Montcalm and Wolfe
- Pontiac's conspiracy

American Literature

- *Longfellow*—"Miles Standish," "Giles Corey," "The Building of the Ship"
- *Hawthorne*—*Grandfather's Chair, The Gentle Boy, Tales of the White Hills, Biographical Stories*
- *Whittier*—"Mabel Martin," "Snowbound," "Among the Hills"
- *Irving*—*The Sketch Book*
- *Hart*—*Source Book of American History* (original source material, four volumes)
- *Moore*—*Pilgrims and Puritans*
- *Baldwin*—*Conquest of the Old Northwest*
- *Franklin*—*Autobiography*
- *Seven American Classics*

- ***Prescott**—The Conquest of Mexico*
- ***Wright**—Children's Stories of American Literature*
- ***Burke**—Conciliation with the American Colonies*

English Literature

- ***Tennyson**—* "The Coming of Arthur," "The Passing of Arthur"
- ***Scott**—* "Lay of the Last Minstrel," "Stories from Waverly"
- ***Dickens**—Child's History of England*
- ***Richardson**—Stories from Old English Poetry*
- ***Lamb**—Tales from Shakespeare*
- ***Church**—Stories from English History*
- ***Morris**—English Historical Tales*
- ***Kendall**—Source Book of English History*
- ***Macaulay**—History of England* (Introduction)
- *Choice English Lyrics*

European Literature

- *Ten Great Events*
- ***Lanier**—Froissart*
- ***Schiller**—William Tell*
- ***Bryant**—* "Iliad" poem
- *Don Quixote*—easy adaptation

Course of Study

The child should be given research assignments about particular aspects of this period of history, and be taught how to use, and cite, reference works. Continue on with writing and oral reporting. Add anything else you wish. Continue with nature study, Bible study and math.

14
Grade Seven

rade seven turns toward Europe, covering the Reformation, the Puritans in England and Louis XIV in France. Geographical study is also primarily European. In the study of the Reformation, you will get to know men like Luther, Leo X, Charles V, Loyola, Gustavus Adolphus and Henry VIII. The Puritan issue was foundational in our early history, perhaps more than any other single event, and needs to be understood. Studying "home first" in this case will look at the simplicity of Puritans in American, then later viewing the more complex issues that brought them to our shores. Their spirit was, and has remained, the American spirit, which is *passion for liberty*. Regarding the French, use the same approach. First study the French in North America under their simple conditions before going back to see the complexity of government and society of the French in France.

American History

The period studied in seventh grade is from 1763-1789. The causes of the Revolution are now examined within the history of England, as well as in the colonies. This will include events leading up to the Revolution, the Revolution itself, and the results that lead to adoption of Constitution. In historical study, rather than repeated surveys year after year, more lasting knowledge will be attained if the child "grows up with" his country, taking it portion by portion, year after year. The child should ideally become one with the motives and impulses—with the very hearts—of our founders, and this can not be achieved by a quick overview such as that which is condensed into a text.

One book that emphasizes how we need to trade the "important" for the crucial in history is Judson's *The Growth of the American Nation*. Another with a focus on the essentials is Mace's *Method in History*. The broad view is what we want, not the tedious details. Although these books supplement a previous store of historical knowledge, do not be tempted to use them as texts. They lack the poetry and passion of real history.

In seventh grade, first look at the causes of the Revolution. This brings in the history of the colonies and the Puritan revolution in England, which brought forth a people passionate for freedom and independence. Their early years in America made them self-reliant and self-governing. As time passed, regulations put a damper on their freedom to trade freely. Many stepped around these English regulations by smuggling. The British saw the financial assets that American offered and, understandably, wanted a "piece of the pie." America—young, a bit wild, bold and having had a luscious taste of freedom—would have nothing to do with oppression of any sort. When we look at the surface, we tend to think that a tea tax was such a minor issue to fight a war over. However, there were much deeper issues here, and reading these suggested works will reveal the underlying causes. Although an important issue was taxation, the emphasis was on *without representation*.

There were Deeper Issues

Comparisons

In studying the colonies and their main characters, you can see differences and similarities. While Samuel Adams embodies the Massachusetts character of Puritanism, Washington—although at first a Virginian with the English character—becomes full American patriot.

The Puritan influence in Europe can be compared with the early struggle for liberty in this country. Some say that the Americans were merely continuing this struggle for rights that began in England. It is amazing to think that today—as during the period of the Revolution—America is fighting not only her own, but the world's battles for freedom. Nothing has really changed. Our innermost character, *thank God,* has remained the same. Burke, in "Conciliation with the Colonies" said:

> *In this character of the Americans, a love of freedom is the predominating feature which marks and distinguishes the whole; and as an ardent is always a jealous affection, your colonies become suspicious, restive and untractable whenever they see the least attempt to wrest from them by force, or shuffle from them by chicane, what they think the only advantage worth living for. . . .*

You may go back to examine life and work of Luther—the Reformation—to see additional foundational work for both religious and political liberty.

Life of Samuel Adams (Hosmer) will give an interesting example of this period in America. The life of Washington is central. You may wish to read portions of Washington Irving's *Life of Washington* (see excerpt in the sixth-grade chapter). Fiske's *War of Independence* is another good choice, as well as Scudder's *Life of Washington,* especially the part dealing with the Revolution.

In the study of the war itself, choose a few important campaigns, events and biographies. Emphasize the sacrifices made, the spirit of the soldiers, as well as the qualities of the leaders, both in the military and in government. You might wish to compare with current events. Use maps.

In history as well as in other subjects, strive for deeper understanding, not mere surface learning. This means you must spend enough time on each topic. Remember, history is your most important subject. Give it its due attention. If you spend two or three weeks on each of the following topics, our foundational history and resulting patriotism will become clear reality in your children's lives. A single noteworthy campaign will impart more than a light overview of all the battles. See the history outline of topics—including major events of the Revolutionary War—at the end of this chapter.

France

This year, you might wish to include Benjamin Franklin's work in France and the contributions of Lafayette. Add further study of French character to the previous year's study of the French people and explorers in Canada, by examining the causes that lead a despotic government (Louis XIV's reign) to aid a freedom fight.

The Constitution

The war was over. Smooth sailing? No way. Studying this period reveals the differences between the colonies and the compromises that brought one nation out of many differing ideas. The discussions were even hostile at times, and agreement was despaired of, and finally was brought forth by the yielding of many. We can relate this study to our daily lives, seeing a practical example of diplomacy in action. Your child will learn to "give and take," a very important life skill. We can come to agreement. We can compromise. We can love.

This "making of a new nation" reminds me of the recent beginnings of free government in Iraq. It is natural to have, as in our beginnings, tendencies toward disunion and anarchy. Yes, we can believe for a good result for Iraq, as was seen our own history—out of chaos, stability.

One of the easiest ways to study the Constitution is, again, to look at the players of this period—Madison, Hamilton, Washington, Franklin.

This year's study should reveal how the previous Articles of Confederation taught lessons for the new government—what worked and what didn't. The Constitution is the epitome of the political history of America. At this point, one can look back and see all previous history leading to a united government under the Constitution.

Remember, you will not cover everything about this period, but what you do cover will be a sufficient foundation for further study and comparisons.

Literature

History and literature go hand in hand, and the literature of this period is rich and abundant. The selections for this period will impart your children with the highest ideals and patriotism. Seventh-grade topics are:

Reformation: Germany, Europe
- Leo X
- Luther
- Charles V
- Henry VIII
- Loyola
- Gustavus Adolphus
- Protestant-Catholic conflict

Puritan Revolution: England
- Charles I and Parliament, Strafford
- Hampden, Pym, Cromwell, Milton
- William of Orange, Protestant succession
- Wesley, Nonconformists

Louis XIV: France
- Royalty, aristocracy
- Tyranny of upper classes
- Lafayette

In former grades the character of the French was seen in Canada. This included customs and religion exemplified by LaSalle, Frontenac, Champlain, Marquette, the Jesuits and others. Some of these have also given insight to the French government and monarchy, notably Champlain, Marquette and the French wars.

American History Outline

The biographies of Washington (Scudder) and Samuel Adams (Hosmer) are fore-most. Other authors' works may be used.

- Causes of Revolution in colonies and in England
- Life of Samuel Adams as Puritan leader
- Revolutionary War
- Boston before evacuation
- Struggle for New York
- Declaration of Independence
- Retreat through New Jersey
- Burgoyne's invasion (S.A. Drake's account)
- Battles at sea: John Paul Jones and others
- Washington at Valley Forge
- Cornwallis' campaign at the South
- Financial condition at close of war
- Life and character of Washington
- Lives of Franklin, Paul Jones, John Adams, Morris
- Hostility between states
- Congress and the Articles of Confederation
- The Constitutional Convention and results
- The life of James Madison, related to Constitution

American Literature

- *Longfellow*—"Paul Revere's Ride," "Evangeline" (for French life and earlier history)
- *Emerson*—"Lexington," "Boston," and other poems
- *Webster*—Bunker Hill, Adams and Jefferson, Speech on the Landing of the Pilgrims, Speech on John Adams
- *Bryant*—"Song of Marion's Men"
- *Lowell*—"Under the Old Elm"
- *Holmes*—"Grandmother's Story of Bunker Hill," "A Ballad of the Boston Tea Party"
- *Camps and Firesides of the Revolution*

- **Coffin**—*Boys of '76*
- *American War Ballads and Lyrics*
- **Moore**—*From Colony to Commonwealth, Life of Benjamin Franklin*
- **Scudder**—*Life of Washington*
- **Hart**—*Source Book of American History,* "Revolution and Confederation"
- **Washington**—*Rules of Conduct* and other papers
- **Franklin**—*Poor Richard's Almanac*
- **Cooper**—*Last of the Mohicans*
- **Wright**—*Stories of American Literature*
- **Sewell**—*Twelve Naval Captains,* first part
- **Fiske and Irving**—*Washington and His Country*
- **Sedgwick**—*Life of Samuel de Champlain*
- **Hapgood**—*Life of John Paul Jones*
- **Warren**—Address
- *Declaration of Independence*
- **Burke**—Speech on the American War
- **Washington**—Letters, Farewell Address, etc.
- **Lanier**—"The Battle of Lexington"
- **Hawthorne**—"Old Ticonderoga"
- **Everett**— Oration on Washington, etc.
- Additional biographies, poems and literature

English Literature

- **Macaulay**—*History of England,* Puritan revolution
- **Hughes**—*Tom Brown's School Days*
- **Dickens**—*The Christmas Carol*
- **Scott**—*Tales of a Grandfather,* Wallace and Bruce
- **Lamb**—*Shakespeare's Tragedies,* historical plays
- **Goldsmith**—*Vicar of Wakefield*
- **Burns**—*Cotter's Saturday Night*
- **Kendall**—*Source Book of English History*
- **Guerber**—*Story of the English,* selected parts

Other European Literature

- **Grote**—*The Two Great Retreats*
- **Shakespeare**—*Merchant of Venice*
- **Plutarch**—*Lives*
- **Motley**—*Life of Peter the Great*
- **White**—*Natural History of Selbourne*
- **Palmer**—*Stories from the Classic Literature of Many Nations*
- **Irving**—*Stories of the Alhambra*
- The Letters of Chesterfield to his Son
- *William Tell*

15
Grade Eight

We have seen American history evolve from the simple to the multi-faceted. Some of the topics covered in this grade are deep and complex. Opinions are often opposing, leaving no clearly-defined "history" of events or topics. This complicates matters, but because of several years of study—line upon line—your child has grown in thoughtfulness, knowledge and patriotism and can come away with the primary ideas fixed in their knowledge store.

History is not merely events that stand alone, but each has an influence on another event, and in this grade particularly, topics are interconnected, therefore easier to comprehend and retain. (We will leave, until the higher grades, more complex issues such as legislation, finance and taxation.)

The theme of eighth-grade study is Westward Expansion under the Constitution, carrying ideas of government, school and society along with the movement of peoples. Improvement in systems of government were needed, as population grew by immigration, and as population spread over at least half of the continent.

History is the concrete example of philosophies and results. It gives the best picture of the effectiveness of decisions made, by the graphic example of the results obtained. It is the test of the correctness of conclusions. If history does not do this, does not inspire judgement, it is not worthy of our time. Thus history is the best morality-building subject.

Some biographies to read this year are those of John Quincy Adams, Daniel Webster and Abraham Lincoln. Adams' life spanned from nearly the beginnings of the nation to the beginnings of the anti-slavery movement. Webster was a great defender of the Constitution. His speeches may be read in seventh and eighth grades as well as in high school. Lincoln was a great leader who rose from the ranks of the "common man" and whose character was perfectly fitted for the times of his service.

If time permits also read biographies of Hamilton, Jefferson, Calhoun, Clay, Fulton, Field, Morse, Garrison, Stephens, Horace Greeley, Whittier, Whitney, Peter Cooper and Sumner.

Using the "home first" principle, if possible, expose your children to local government, and even service such as working in political campaigns. Teach other principles from known things. Knowledge of basic economics can begin from something as simple as a lemonade stand, or being responsible for the family's accounting.

Texts

Texts actually can be used, but not as primary learning material. Instead, use them for your general framework, perhaps as a checkpoint, to see what you may have missed. However, remember that not *everything* needs to be covered. You may also use brief excerpts from texts as either an introduction, or summary, of the period studied. Another use is to build a timeline with the dates in the text or to chose a few of the most important to memorize.

Other Tools

Maps, outline maps, museums, collections, PBS, The History Channel and videos may also be used. Their use is more effective if limited to only the portion that applies to the topic at hand. Outline maps can be purchased from: ***www.knowledgequestmaps.com***

American History Outline

- Hamilton and the finances, banking system
- Early political parties, origin and growth
- Growth in territory (use maps)
- War of 1812
- Internal improvements, routes westward
- Immigraton, character and events
- Jackson and the spoils system
- Inventions, influence on progress
- Growth, history of slavery
- Mexican War, motives and results
- California gold rush
- States' rights doctrine, southern leaders
- Civil War plan, most important campaigns
- System of revenue, national debt
- Three departments of government, checks and balances
- Civil-service reform, review of spoils system

Some of the highlights of this period were:

- The first telegram
- Completion of the railroad to the Pacific
- Lincoln at Gettysburg
- Grant and Lee at Appomattox

European History

- Julius Caesar and Augustus: The Roman Empire
- The French Revolution compared with the American Revolution
- England's conquest of India. Clive and Hastings
- The English in Africa. Livingstone and Stanley
- Later struggles for Africa
- Revolt of Spanish-America
- Greek war of independence: Turkey and decay of power

- The union of the north German states: Bismarck and King William
- The union of the Italian states: Cavour and Victor Emanuel.
- Queen Victoria's reign: Bright, Gladstone
- Later history of England

American Literature

- **Scudder**—*Masterpieces of American Literature*
- *Nature Pictures by American Poets*
- **Webster**—Speech on Washington
- **Washington**—Farewell Address
- **Longfellow**—"Tales of a Wayside Inn"
- **Emerson**— "Fortune of the Republic," "American Scholar"
- **Schurz**— "Abraham Lincoln," others
- **Lincoln**—Inaugural and other speeches
- **Holmes**— "My Hunt after the Captain"
- **Lowell**—"Bigelow Papers"
- **Stowe**—*Uncle Tom's Cabin*
- **Webster**—The Great Debate (Speech in Reply to Hayne)
- **Burke**—On Conciliation with the American Colonies
- **Parkman**—Oregon Trail
- **Hart**—*Source Book of American History* (latter part)
- **Hawthorne**—*The House of the Seven Gables*
- **Guerber**—*Story of the Great Republic* (latter part)
- **Vedder**—*American Writers of Today*
- **Cooper**—*The Pilot*
- **Sewell**—*Twelve Naval Captains*
- *Great Words from Great Americans*
- *Poems of American Patriotism*
- Hymns and patriotic songs

English Literature

- **Addison**—*Roger de Coverley*
- **Scott**—*Lady of the Lake, Marmion*
- **Goldsmith**—*The Deserted Village, Traveller*
- **Scott**—*Ivanhoe, The Abbot, Rob Roy*
- **Macaulay**—Essay on Samuel Johnson
- **Kendall**—*Source Book of English History*
- **Dickens**—*Tale of Two Cities*
- *Seven British Classics*

Other European Literature

- **Shakespeare**—*Julius Caesar*
- **Martineau**—*Peasant and Prince*
- **Plato**—*The Judgment of Socrates*
- **Guerber**—*Story of the Romans*
- **Browning**— "Pied Piper" and others
- **Plutarch**—*Lives*
- **Cervantes**—*Don Quixote*
- *Two Great Retreats*
- **Scott**—*The Talisman* and *Quentin Durward*
- **Hugo**—*Les Miserables*
- **Motley**—*Peter the Great, The Siege of Leydon*

With study of even some of the preceding suggested titles, your eighth-grade graduate will have a better grasp of wisdom and knowledge than even many of today's high-school graduates.

Part 2

Introduction

Since *Easy Homeschooling* is a literary method, in the first part of this book, I provide specific suggestions for each grade level through eighth grade, particularly in history, which is one of the two most important subjects. What about the other subjects?

Because I previously detailed basic *Easy Homeschooling* techniques for nearly every subject in my first two books, *Easy Homeschooling Techniques* and *Easy Homeschooling Companion,* and because with "easy" there really is nothing more to share (or that you have to do), I invited guest authors to contribute to this section of this book. These authors have great ideas and a lot of experience both in education and in homeschooling. Some cover topics I did not cover, such as keyboarding. They all use their ideas to add variety, interest and creativity to your homeschooling.

Reading and writing are the pillars of *Easy Homeschooling,* so I happily include three guest chapters on these subjects. I left off with eighth grade and Janice Campbell continues on with her literature suggestions for high school. Former homeschooled student, Rachel Starr Thomson, gives us a delightful piece on adding spark to writing, while Kim Kautzer helps us build a "fire" under reluctant writers, with lots of ideas for this subject.

I personally edited these chapters to insure the *Easy Homeschooling* standard. I desire that the reader always have easy-to-understand, easy-to-use information. For detailed instructions for many aspects of homeschooling, including some mentioned in this section of *Easy Homeschooling Curriculum,* go to my previous two books, noted above.

16
Teaching Writing

By Kim Kautzer

I t should have been so easy. After all, you weren't asking for much—just a story or something. To simplify things, you didn't even care how long it should be. Or what topic he picked. Given a lot of freedom, you reasoned, he wouldn't feel so squished or frustrated, and the words would just flow.

So what went wrong?

Your plan backfired miserably, and now your son hunches tearfully over a mountain of wadded pages, each one a smudged and wrinkled reminder of what he already believes about himself: *I can't write!*

If it's any comfort, you're not alone. This scene plays out at kitchen tables and makeshift schoolrooms around the country, where dejected students scrunch up papers, break pencils, bang keyboards and cry buckets—and disheartened moms throw up their hands in frustration. Maybe it helps to know that homeschoolers everywhere share the same lament: *Why is writing so hard to teach?*

For one thing, parents often feel insecure, inadequate and unequipped. Teaching writing, a dreaded chore, ranks right up there with a trip to the dentist. Although we know the importance of passing on good writing skills to our children, a stack of excuses stands in the way:

- How can I teach if I never learned to write?
- Writing comes easily to me—but I don't have a clue how to teach my kids.
- I don't know what to expect from their writing.
- I don't know how to grade a paper.
- I haven't found a writing program I like.

Your own shortcomings are enough to make you less than eager to assign writing. But your kids' negative reactions to your teaching attempts can cause you to abandon the subject all together. After all, who loves to face the tearful outbursts or sullen expressions that writing assignments can produce?

Kids are often paralyzed by writer's block, fear and perfectionism. Most want to write a paper once and call it done. Not only that, they expect you to rave over it and accept it as a finished product! The smallest hint of an idea from Mom sets off howls of protest.

Why can't I leave it this way? You never like anything I write!

Insecure parent, reluctant child, blank paper. Three ingredients that, combined together, fairly promise that your hopes for teaching writing will fail. Let's face it. It's easy to keep pushing writing to the back burner with plans of getting to it "someday." And for many, someday has come and gone, and now you have

- a high schooler who can't write;
- a panicked mom burdened by guilt;
- and the infernal blank page that taunts you both.

Stumbling Blocks

Plenty of stumbling blocks stand in the way of a young writer's success. Laziness, procrastination and perfectionism interfere with motivation and productivity. Anticipation of parental criticism creates unrealistic anxiety. Lack of direction or poor writing skills affect confidence and performance.

But take heart—these stumbling blocks are not so heavy that they can't be moved, or so high that they can't be scaled! Start simply with some of these ideas:

- *Establish limits.* When you set limits—such as giving step-by-step directions for the writing project—your children will feel more secure in their efforts. Provide concrete help by way of checklists, brainstorming worksheets or skill-building exercises.
- *Expand skills.* Start by introducing students to the thesaurus so they can choose more vivid, descriptive, or concrete words. As they make stronger word choices, not only will their vocabulary improve, their writing will begin to sparkle as well. In addition, teach them to incorporate grammar concepts into their writing. Are they learning about prepositional phrases, for instance? Have them use one in a current composition.
- *Offer variety.* If your kids' writing diet consists mainly of boring book reports, change things up a bit! Here are some ideas for doing that.

Descriptive

Descriptive writing lessons help students use their senses to zoom in on details—the crunch of golden leaves underfoot; the rich, buttery aroma of sugar cookies browning in the oven; the mournful howl of a winter gust as it whips through barren branches.

Informative

Informative writing can include biographies, news articles, recipes, advice columns, short reports, instruction manuals, and more. As students get older, persuasive essays and research papers should be introduced as well.

Narrative

Narrative writing can take students well beyond the mundane memoirs of last summer's vacation! Students can interview someone and write a narrative of an emotional event. They can retell a simple fable or Bible story from the perspective of one of the characters. For additional variety, introduce personification by asking them to write a story from the first-person point of view of an object. "I Am a Mirror" or "I, Weedwhacker" can inspire some lively prose!

Introducing the Writing Process

Though it may sound freeing, writing about "whatever you want" can actually frustrate struggling writers, so start by recommending concrete topics they can choose from. Instead of saying, "Write about a food," suggest they use their five senses to describe a taco, a cinnamon roll or an ice cream sundae.

Next, position them for success by setting boundaries for the composition. For example, limit its length to one paragraph of five to seven sentences.

Most importantly, teach your kids that writing is a *process*, not a one-time event. Children trained in the process of writing learn to view the final draft as merely one of several steps in an evolving work. And when the steps seem doable, even the most intimidated writer stands a chance at accomplishment.

As you take your kids through the writing process, provide a plan or schedule to follow. Don't allow your procrastinators to do all the steps in one day; there's wisdom in letting a composition rest between revisions. Furthermore, don't impose the demands of the writing process on every single composition—it's enough for one writing project at a time to go through several revisions.

Break up such assignments into five manageable steps:

1. ***Brainstorming*** gets ideas flowing so your student has something to say. He might brainstorm for a how-to composition by listing the steps of the process. If he's writing a descriptive paragraph, he must carefully study the subject for interesting details. For a narrative, he'll want to list events in order. Whatever the topic, suggest a brainstorming method—mind map, list or outline, for instance—that's best for the kind of composition he's writing.

2. ***Sloppy Copy.*** This is the imperfect, flawed rough draft. It doesn't have to be neat—just legible! As the student writes, he'll draw from the many ideas gathered during brainstorming. If he still can't think of things to say, he may need to brainstorm even more. Have him skip lines so there's room to edit later.

3. ***Self-Editing and Revising.*** You'll quickly find that students don't like to edit their papers. Unfortunately, by not proofreading their own papers thoroughly, they place themselves in a no-win situation; that is, they're too lazy to edit their own work carefully, yet they fall apart when they see all the changes you suggest!

Does this sound familiar?

I don't like editing. It takes too much time. Besides, I like my paper just the way it is. It sounds good to me. Anyway, if I don't worry about it, Mom will find my mistakes. Why go to all the time and trouble to find mistakes (and—gasp!—correct them) when someone else will do it for me?

However, when their parent-edited composition comes back, they sing a different tune!

My paper is too marked up. I thought it was fine. You're always so critical! I can't do anything right. I didn't see all that stuff when I read it!

Self-editing plays an important role in the writing process and shouldn't be neglected. Why? It helps the student take more responsibility for his own progress. Instead of depending solely on you for assistance, he must make some changes before you ever see the paper.

Ideally, he should use some sort of checklist as a guide, helping him identify errors in content, style and mechanics. As he compares his rough draft to the checklist, he makes corrections and improvements. The rewritten paper he turns in to you—the first revision—will then be ready for your inspection.

4. ***Parent Editing.*** Every paper benefits from a second opinion. Only after your child has had a chance to self-edit and rewrite should you offer your own advice. Don't let this scare you! The more you edit and revise your kids' papers, the easier it will become. Familiarity produces recognition. You'll quickly become skilled at spotting repeated words, passive writing and misplaced modifiers. At first, however, you might have to hunt for them. Using an impartial checklist helps you to be objective and lets you comment on the work without condemning the child. Not only that, it takes the pressure and guesswork out of editing. And because your student knows what you expect, he responds more positively to suggestions for improvement. Along with tips, include plenty of positive feedback. Find ways to bless his efforts; then make gentle suggestions that encourage growth without squishing his spirit.

5. ***Final Draft.*** Now for the last step in the process—the final draft—where the student makes corrections based on your comments and

puts the finishing touches on his paper. This is the one he'll be proud to mail to Grandma, post on the fridge or publish in your support group's newsletter. When he compares this polished version to his very first draft, what a difference he'll see! And though he may never love the process that has brought him to this point, at least he'll learn to respect it.

Inch by Inch, It's a Cinch

Teaching writing doesn't have to be hard. But perhaps you feel insecure, so writing may not be happening in your home. In that case, seek out a program that offers strong support for the parent. Good programs offer clear instructions and checklists, as well as editing and grading tips, and will help you feel better equipped to teach writing—and when you radiate confidence, your kids pick up on it.

And speaking of kids, remember that most want to make the leap from blank paper to final draft in one stride. Yet when they realize their target is more reachable by taking smaller steps, they begin to believe they can do it. And in the end they achieve a worthy goal—a polished composition they're proud to share with others.

Kim Kautzer, veteran homeschooler and author, loves to help parents feel more confident about teaching writing. She is the co-author of *WriteShop: An Incremental Writing Program,* honored as one of Cathy Duffy's *100 Top Picks for Homeschool Curriculum.* You may reach Kim at kim@writeshop.com or visit her website:

www.writeshop.com

17

Writing Vividly

By Rachel Starr Thomson

anguage is a many-splendored thing. It's also very useful. Without it, you couldn't read this chapter. And we'd all be communicating by grunting and pointing.

Sadly, language is swiftly slipping away from the people of this country. Gone are the days when greed was "avarice," lack was "penury," and "the Poet" referred to Shakespeare or Robbie Burns and not to the penner of the immortal,

Roses are red

Violets are blue

You look like a monkey

And you smell like one, too.

As a dedicated guardian of language, I stand with my finger in the dam of ignorance and hope to stem the tide. Homeschoolers are and should be among the faithful, but these days we can use all the help we can get. For this reason I offer the following guide to descriptive writing. Enjoy your romp through the lilies of language.

The Dissection of an Essay

The first thing to do in writing is to write. Figure out what you want to say and say it, no matter how badly. Once the words are on paper they are fair game for the dreaded red pen, and the repressed surgeon in you is free to come out.

For the purposes of discussion, I submit the following essay, entitled, "My Day." This is the sort of writing project homeschoolers are constantly being coerced into composing, more's the pity. They ought to be writing treatises on Fairyland, poetic guides to the zoo, and tales of flowers, fancy, and farce (not to forget cabbages and kings). Most people, however, stick to the mundane in their choosing of topics, so for this chapter I shall do so as well.

My Day
By Rachel Thomson

Today I woke up. Then I got dressed. Upstairs, the girls got dressed, too. We came into the kitchen and said good morning. We had pancakes for breakfast.

After breakfast I went in the basement and started working. I researched folk music for our "Frontier Days" unit study curriculum. Then I took my manuscript for Theodore Pharris Saves the Universe *and went outside and edited it and spilled my tea on it and got cold, went inside, ate something, typed, got writer's block, and stopped working for a little while.*

I don't remember if I ate lunch.

I emailed Carolyn and Sandy and then I worked on Hopelessly Homeschooled. *After that I went upstairs and ate supper. Then I cleaned the kitchen.*

When I am finished with this essay I will go to bed.

The above is dreadful, but it is not beyond help. A pen, joined with imagination and some literary discipline, can turn even "My Day" into a masterpiece.

Reading Between the Lines

Whenever you find yourself turning out a story that is drab and colourless, it is highly advisable to go back and read between the lines of your own writing—search, in other words, for the stories hidden within the mundane outline. When the stories-within-the-story have been unearthed, it is time to bring them into the light for the benefit of the reader. Three things will help you do this.

Inner Perspective

First, look for *inner perspective.* In an essay such as "My Day," you are not writing the story of a lampshade. You are writing the story of a person; the person, in fact, whom you know most about—yourself. You felt a certain way about everything you did, from getting up to going to bed. Dredge your memory for your thoughts and feelings, and bring them to the surface. Doing so will turn a partridge of a passage into a nightingale; it will make your prose sing.

Just look at the effect inner perspective has on the first line of "My Day":

> **Today I woke up.** *As I remember it, I was not happy to get up. My alarm clock is a sadistic little object with a way of boring a hole through my head with its never-ending beep-beep-beep.*

This brings up a wonderful element of story, called "conflict." None of us likes conflict in real life, but a story devoid of it is a story devoid of interest. No one cares if Joe Hero wants to cross a mud puddle. If the mud puddle is full of alligators, then we care. If Joe Hero's true love is on the other side, dying of poison for which Joe carries the antidote, then we care even more. You see? Conflict. Don't leave bed without it.

The sentence from "My Day," then, employs feelings and conflict. It expands to several sentences and becomes:

Today I awoke to the incessant ringing of my alarm clock. I closed my eyes and dreamt of a land where princesses are awakened by the light tickle of butterfly's wings, but I was forced out of bed and fairyland by my alarm beeping a hole through my brain.

Detail

The second thing that will help you draw out the story-within-your-story is *detail*. Sherlock Holmes once asked Dr. Watson if he had ever seen the staircase down the hall. "Of course I've seen it," Dr. Watson said, rather indignantly. "I walk up and down it every day." "Then tell me," pressed Holmes, "How many steps are there?"

Dr. Watson, of course, had no idea. He had seen the staircase a thousand times without ever *really* seeing it. Sentences like "I got dressed" tell the reader nothing except that you sometimes wear clothes. If you use detail, you can use this scene to communicate a great deal about yourself. Most of us cannot remember the number of steps in a staircase, but there are a great many details we do remember. Use those details that come to mind and make a habit of noticing others, so that your writing will continue to improve.

I stumbled out of bed and walked into my dresser. The pain of that collision helped me clear my brain. Ah yes, time to get dressed. Mentally, I thought over my day. No, I had nowhere to go—and I had a great deal of writing to do. That meant one thing: dress for comfort.

I pulled on my baggy plaid pajamas, an oversized grey t-shirt, and a small, unbuttoned purple sweater. My feet were cold, so I snugly immersed them in pink socks and brown loafers. I left the room, reflecting that it might be wise to avoid mirrors for the day.

Atmosphere

The third thing that will help turn a "yawnable" essay into a real atten-tion-getter is atmosphere. This is closely linked with detail and inner perspective, and involves communicating with all five senses of your reader. No, I am not suggesting that you place a scratch-'n-sniff in the center of your essay. I am saying that people take in the world around them through every sense that God has given them, and if you want them to enter *your* world, give them a chance to see, hear, feel, smell and taste it.

Watch as the end of the first paragraph as "My Day" is transformed via inner perspective, detail, and atmosphere:

Upstairs, the girls got dressed, too. We came into the kitchen and said good morning. We had pancakes for breakfast.

becomes . . .

Meanwhile, up two flights of stairs and over the wreckage of the little kids' play area, my sisters were also getting dressed. Deborah was the last to float gracefully down the stairs, nar-rowly avoiding a tumble at the bottom where her toe con-nected with a wooden replica of the Tower of Babel and sent the pieces into eternal confusion. She wore a black, slightly flared pair of pants, a red v-neck top, chunky sandals, and makeup. Her hair glowed with the well-pampered sheen of tresses which have been parked in front of a mirror for the last hour, holding tryst with a curling iron.

Deborah and I convened in the kitchen where the aroma of frying batter and syrup announced that pancakes were waiting. We loaded up our plates and those of our little "part-ners," pausing to say "Good morning," eye each other, and wonder if we could possibly be related.

Adjectives and Whistles

Let's have a look at the next two paragraphs, shall we?

> *After breakfast I went in the basement and started working.*
> *I researched folk music for our "Frontier Days" unit study*
> *curriculum. Then I took my manuscript for* Theodore Pharris
> Saves the Universe *and went outside and edited it and spilled*
> *my tea on it and got cold, went inside, ate something, typed,*
> *got writer's block, and stopped working for a little while.*
> *I don't remember if I ate lunch.*

You may have noticed in the editing of the previous passages that a great number of descriptive words were employed. Forget "pants, socks, and shoes"—these are all eminently forgettable. *Plaid* pants, *pink* socks, and *brown* loafers improve the scene dramatically. There is no limit to what an adjective can do.

Do not tell me that you work in your basement; I don't care, because all I know is that it is a basement. If you tell me about it, I may take interest. Is your basement cold and dank? Is it bright and sunny? Is it dark as a tomb? Lonely as a church on Tuesday morning? Tell me!

Adjectives

create

Atmosphere

My basement, in which I work and sleep, is cold, dark, and well-trodden by booted little feet that pass in and out of the sliding doors all day. If I tell you so, I create atmosphere, and you are that much further into my world.

And did I "research folk music"? "For our Frontier Days unit study curriculum," did I say? Be it known that "research folk music" involves a blood-chilling hunt through hundreds of internet files, chasing down likely suspects, throwing away irrelevant leads, listening to thousands of MIDI files. It involves hauling the rare prize in for inclusion in a manuscript that must be finished in thirty days, and takes about five years worth of effort.

Now, to the next sentence. This sentence suffers from abuse by a writer with a runny pen. Have you ever taken part in gym class? Do you know what it is like to run on the spot for an hour, waiting in vain for the sound of a whistle to tell you that you may stop? A period is a whistle. The third sentence in the above paragraph has been running too long, and is desperately in need of a breather. Have mercy. Blow the whistle. Use a period.

The second paragraph (fourth sentence) is just fine. I like it. A nice, ironic, simple sentence makes a wonderful change from the heady world of adjectives, emotions, and detail. So go ahead, be a minimalist once in a while. A change is as good as a rest. Just make sure you don't indulge in that philosophy to such an extent that you put your readers to sleep.

Characters

> *I emailed Carolyn and Sandy and then I worked on* Hopelessly Homeschooled. *After that I went upstairs and ate supper. Then I cleaned the kitchen.*
> *When I am finished with this essay I will go to bed.*

The introduction of characters in a piece of writing adds instant variety and all sorts of potential for fun. A note of caution: you should never bring people into your writing without describing them in some way so that your reader knows who they are. Neglecting to do so is like neglecting to introduce friends; it's rude. Such descriptions can be very simple ("my sister Deborah") or very complex ("my cousin Carolyn, a dancer who talks like Shakespeare and terrorizes the young men of her sphere.")

The other lines in "My Day" can be dealt with according to all of the principles and techniques already described. One thing remains to be discussed:

Slash and Burn

Writing is a craft. Just as a blacksmith, consummate craftsman that he is, must pulverize the iron that he shapes, so a writer must not be too soft on his writing. As I said earlier, the first step in writing is to spit it all out on paper. Then, take the shapeless mass that results and form it into something worthy of attention.

When this is done, it is time for the writer's version of hammer and tongs—the red pen. Edit, edit, edit. Unnecessary words are wearisome; slash them. Keep good details, burn superfluous ones. Reshape misspellings and sentence structures until they behave according to law. Finally, look for information that is a burden on the story and remove it. Your readers should feel as though they are cutting through blue Caribbean waters, not slogging through quicksand.

Here follows the final version of "My Day." If it makes you feel better about attacking your own prose, feel free to take an axe to mine. What would you change? The answer may tell you a great deal about your own style, and help you discover the unique writing voice that belongs to you.

My Day

By Rachel Thomson

Today I awoke to the incessant ringing of my alarm clock. I closed my eyes and dreamt of a land where princesses are awakened by the light tickle of butterfly's wings, but I was forced out of bed and fairyland by my alarm beeping a hole through my brain.

I stumbled out of bed and walked into my dresser. The pain of that collision helped me clear my brain. Ah yes, time to get dressed. Mentally, I thought over my day. No, I had nowhere to go—and I had a great deal of writing to do. That meant one thing: dress for comfort.

I pulled on my baggy plaid pajamas, an oversized grey t-shirt, and a small, unbuttoned purple sweater. My feet were cold, so I snugly immersed them in pink socks and brown loafers. I left the room, reflecting that it might be wise to avoid mirrors for the day.

Meanwhile, up two flights of stairs and over the wreckage of the little kids' play area, my sisters were also getting dressed. Deborah was the last to float gracefully down the stairs, narrowly avoiding a tumble at the bottom where her toe connected with a wooden replica of the Tower of Babel and sent the pieces into eternal confusion. She wore a black, slightly flared pair of pants, a red v-neck top, chunky sandals, and makeup. Her hair glowed with the well-pampered sheen of tresses which have been parked in front of a mirror for the last hour, holding tryst with a curling iron.

Deborah and I convened in the kitchen where the aroma of frying batter and syrup announced that pancakes were waiting. We loaded up our plates and those of our little "partners," pausing to say "Good morning," eye each other, and wonder if we could possibly be related.

When breakfast was over, I descended into the pit to work. The "pit" is our basement. It houses a thrift store's worth of junk, my bedroom, and a computer that groans like the ghost of Jacob Marley. During the day it is less a pit than at night; for a pair of glass sliding doors, which one can reach by following a kid-tracked trail of mud, lead out into the yard and let the sun in. Even so, the winter's chill is not yet gone from the basement, and I work in it at the risk of my fingers and toes.

Once on the computer, I lost myself in a fog of writing. I tracked research through dank bogs of internet links and leads, every now and then finding a treasure and hauling it out into the light. When I finished with that process, I turned to red-inking a children's manuscript called Theodore Pharris Saves the Universe, *which wormed its way out of my author's mind when I was fourteen and is now about to be published. My nineteen-year-old mind is appalled at the idea, and so the manuscript demands my time and attention in the editing department.*

I left the long dark of the basement and worked with pen and paper outside on the poky grass on the edge of our yard, where the spring rains are dry and Lake Mud has not encroached.

I don't remember if I ate lunch.

Later in the day writer's block attacked. Words came only in fits and starts, promising to rush in with floods of inspiration as soon as I got to bed. I wrote a letter to Carolyn, my second cousin, a companion as dear as anyone can be who lives three thousand miles away and can be communicated with only through a computer screen. Words flowed out into the letter and ceased again when I signed off.

Thus, I leave this essay and betake myself to the land of inspiration and butterfly wings, where I shall await the coming of another day.

Rachel Starr Thomson *is a homeschool graduate, the oldest of twelve children, and a professional wordsmith. You can find writing tips, devotionals, family-focused essays, fiction and nonfiction books, blogs, and more on her Web site:*

www.LittleDozen.com

18
Speech

By JoJo Tabares

A word fitly spoken is like apples of gold in pictures of silver.
—Proverbs 25:11

Communication skills are vital—especially in the information age. Studies show that effective communicators are happier, do better in school, are more successful and make more money than their less eloquent counterparts. So how do you teach your children to express themselves better? The *fun* way!

Teaching Younger Children

The best way to teach children anything is to make it fun and involve as many of their five senses as possible. Here are some ideas that will foster effective communication skills in your children.

Play Telephone

The more the merrier. This old elementary school game is a delightfully fun way to develop your child's listening skills. This game is perfect for any age. Begin with a simpler message for the younger children and gradually increase the size and complexity as they get older.

Directions to Fun

Have your older child write out directions from your house to somewhere fun, for example, the ice cream shop. Preferably give the directions to a third party who is unfamiliar with the area, and have him follow the directions precisely. Did you get there? If so, have an ice cream cone! If not, talk about what went wrong in the communication. What could be changed that would help get you there the next time? This is a wonderful exercise to help children from fourth through twelfth grades learn to give better directions. But it also is a lesson in itself about communication. In order to effectively communicate what you want, you must learn to say what you mean so that others can fully understand.

Dress for Success

Go to the store or any other public place dressed in your Sunday best. Notice how you are treated. Next go to the same store or a similar location dressed shabbily or inappropriately for the occasion; for example, go to a Mercedes dealership in old jeans and a worn out T-shirt. Notice how differently you are treated. This illustrates that even nonverbal communication has consequences. You will want to point

out a strange person walking on the street and do a little of what I call "brain washing." Paint a picture of the consequences of the communication that is sent when people wear skimpy clothes or dress like hoodlums. Tell them what their choice of clothes is saying to the average person or to a prospective employer. Give them the facts on how this will impact their lives a year, two years and ten years down the line. Tell them what could happen tomorrow if someone draws a conclusion, based on those clothes, that puts them in harm's way.

Talk 'n Listen

Have your child sing Yankee Doodle while another person recites the Pledge of Allegiance. See how long they can go without flubbing it up. If your child can do this too easily, have each one read from a different book. Tell them to each take turns relating what the other had read. This helps illustrate that old saying that God gave us two ears and one mouth in order that we listen twice as much as we talk.

"Um" Contest

Have your child talk about a familiar topic. Any topic. For example, his favorite activity or book. See how long he can keep from uttering "um," "er," "uh," "like" or "ya know." This develops the child's confidence as well as eloquence. Eliminating these "words" in your child's vocabulary will cause the him to focus on becoming more articulate as well as increasing his vocabulary.

Feed Me Applesauce

Blindfold someone and have that person feed applesauce to another blindfolded person. Have a third person who is not blindfolded giving the directions to both parties. This teaches students to give directions more effectively.

Note: This is messy! Fun, but messy! You will want to make sure that your children are not wearing their good clothes and that this activity takes place on a bare floor and not carpet.

Presentation

Have your child give a presentation to a local retirement home. This can include giving a craft demonstration, playing piano as in a short recital, singing or reciting a poem. This teaches your child how to present himself. This can be done with children of all ages. The sooner you get your child comfortable talking in public, the better. It will become like second nature to them and they may be able to avoid the biggest fear that most people have: *public speaking.* Studies show that people who enjoy speaking in public are more successful than those who do not. So get them out there showing off the talents God gave them!

What's Going on in the Picture

This one is great for the little ones. Have your child tell you what he sees in a picture. Encourage him to describe the scenery, the people, the colors—anything he sees. For older children, have them talk about what they think might have happened just before this scene and what they think will happen after. This gives them practice in formulating ideas in a logical manner that others can easily understand.

Finish a Story

This one is also very good for different age groups. Kids love stories! You start off a story and have your child finish it. For very young children, you can tell them a nursery rhyme and have them make up an alternate ending or add on to the story. This exercise is great for teaching beginning verbal communication skills.

Note from Lorraine: This is a great idea to teach creativity in both speaking and writing. When Daughter Jessica was about four, she told a very interesting and lengthy story that I was fortunate enough to tape.

Impromptu Speech

This exercise is wonderful for children of all ages. Pick a topic that your child is familiar with (or just loves) and ask him to speak for about two minutes on that topic. After a while, have your student graduate to speaking on more difficult topics and for longer periods of time. You can start them off by talking about their favorite movie and eventually graduate them to controversial topics like prayer in school.

Lee Iacocca said, "You can have brilliant ideas, but if you can't get them across, they won't get you anywhere." The more your children practice communication skills, the more effective they will be in communicating their needs and ideas. The more fun you can make it, the more they will want to practice these essential skills.

Teaching Older Children

Eighty-seven percent of what we do all day long is communication related. It was such an important skill that the Lord saw fit to include the topic in His Word many times over. Successful communicators make successful people because it touches almost every single aspect of our lives from personal to professional. Here are seven things that all successful communicators know and practice. You can teach these basics to your older children.

The First Rule of Communication

It is the speaker's job to be understood and *not the listener's job to understand*. If you understand this very important principle, it will help you avoid much misunderstanding and frustration. Many people mistakenly assume that, once they say something, it is the listener's job to figure out what they meant. When the listener does not, they say things like, "I just told you!" or they repeat the same statement (perhaps louder, as if the listener was hard of hearing; or slower, as if the listener was lacking a few brain cells). If you understand that it is your job to get your message across, you will take more care to put things clearly. You will be much more forgiving if someone doesn't understand you the first time, or you will find some other way to say it, ensuring the other person will better understand .

Build a Large Vocabulary

There is a reason your teachers and parents were so concerned that you learn your vocabulary words! The bigger your vocabulary, the more ammunition you have in your arsenal with which to make yourself understood. Someone with a large vocabulary can choose to speak plainly for clarity or to speak with technically accurate terminology to relate to those who are more knowledgeable in that field. (Also see Mr. McCabe's chapter on buidling vocabulary.)

Know Your Audience

Effective communicators express themselves well because they have learned to speak to their unique audience (whether one, or a crowd). One size does *not* fit all! That applies just as much to communication as it does to clothing. As a woman of five feet and no inches, a very tiny waist and not so tiny hips and thighs; I can tell you that not all clothes fit me either! My body is unique and so is the way I look at the world.

However, I am not unique in my uniqueness! God created each one of us special. No two people see things exactly the same way. Why do you think police officers will tell you that they can have ten witnesses to a crime and come up with eleven different stories! The more you know about your listeners the more you will be able to relate to them. Some things you will be able to determine by observing their behavior, and some things you may need to ask them. Nobody likes being treated as "one of the crowd." Speak to people as if they are precious and unique children of God!

Be a Good Listener

Most people think of great communicators as talkers, but in reality, they are great listeners! It isn't the guy who is always talking that you love to be around. It's the one who listens to *you!* It's the special friend who always asks how you are and really *wants* the answer! It's the sales girl who wants to sell you what you are *looking* for and not what she has in stock. These are the great communicators! Listening is a critical skill that allows you to know your audience.

Be Confident and Inspiring to Others

What drew people to Ronald Reagan? What was it that Dr. Martin Luther King Jr. had that inspired others? What was it that even Adolph Hitler had that allowed his evil to flourish for a time? It was more than just their words! It's what some call charisma. They were confident in themselves and what they believed. The passion of the speaker came through the message. Your passion will inspire others.

Back up Your Claims with Facts

Asserting a position does not make it so. In order to convince others, especially those who hold another belief, you need more than just your say-so! You need a little thing many politicians today forget to include in their communication: *facts!* Opinions are not very convincing, even when they belong to someone who is an expert in that field! Back up your statements with, "Just the facts, ma'am!" No matter how persuasive your argument may sound, it will never convince that segment of people who start out thinking you are wrong, unless you have something to support your claim beyond "because I say so!" It didn't work for your mother, what makes you think it will work for you?

Understand that Credibility is Vital

What constitutes a fact? According to *Webster's Dictionary*, a fact is a piece of information presented as having objective reality. When successful communicators speak, they present facts that their audience will see as having credibility. Trying to prove abortion rights by quoting Planned Parenthood will not sway anyone who is pro-life. Planned Parenthood is not objective and therefore holds no credibility with the pro-lifer. By the same token, trying to prove a pro-life stance to those who are not Christians will not work by quoting the Bible.

Highly successful people are highly successful communicators. They take responsibility for their message, build an arsenal of words, understand their audience, listen more than they speak, exude confidence and back up their claims with credible facts. You and your children can become more effective communicators!

JoJo Tabares *holds a degree in Speech Communication. Her Christian and humorous approach to communication skills has made her a sought-after speaker. JoJo's articles have appeared in various homeschool magazines and websites such as www.drlaura.com. Her* Say What You Mean *curriculum is endorsed by* The Old Schoolhouse Magazine. *For more information, please visit:*

http://www.ArtofEloquence.com

19
Bible

By Robin Khoury

During my sixteen-plus years of homeschooling, I taught the Bible to my boys by various means. When they were really young we read Bible-story picture books along with the Bible. We memorized Bible verse songs and made charts of verses learned. Somewhere along the way we started reading straight through the Bible. In high school we used a college-credit Old Testament and New Testament video series, among other things. While there is value in all of the above methods, I have come across a Bible study idea recently that I wish I had known about when my boys were younger. And to think, it was sitting on my shelf all the time! The method I'm talking about is a three-pronged approach to Bible study given to me by Great Granddaddy Godsoe who was a Baptist Preacher for sixty-five years.

He was Dr. Godsoe to others, Graddaddy to me. After he died, I happened upon my Granny's (his daughter's) house one day during a cleaning spree. There were approximately forty old dirty notebooks stashed in a box. These notebooks contained all of Grandaddy's Bible studies that he had written during his later years. I rescued them, cleaned them off and stored them in my hall cabinet. I knew they were precious, but I was just so busy homeschooling that I didn't take time to read them. Now that my boys are in college, I peruse the books from time to time. And guess what I found? A wonderful way for homeschool families to study the Bible!

Graddaddy's Three-Way Bible Learning Method

The old notebooks contained three different ways of teaching the Bible in order to get a good overview of the book. These ways are: learning the Bible through studying 1) the major events, 2) characters and 3) places. Once you have these lists, it is easy to use the framework to build a series of family devotions or homeschool Bible studies on them. If you want the students to understand the scope and sequence of the Bible, I suggest keeping your studies fairly simple to begin with. Then as the children get older, you can use the same framework and go more in depth. There are several widely available homeschooling resources on how to plan a unit study which might be helpful if you wish to expand beyond the enrichment ideas at the end of this chapter.

Use the Bible as Your Text

The Bible is the textbook for these lessons. You may find a concordance to be helpful also. (For a wonderful free online searchable Bible see *www.biblegateway.com* .) You can search for topics and words to put together your readings. After you read about an event, character or place from the Bible, you can add enrichment books from your own collection or the library.

How to Teach the Bible Using Principle Events

The following list of the major events of the Bible will give your students a broad overview of the sweep of Scripture. Read selections from the passages, then choose enrichment activities to complement your studies. You may wish to make note cards of all of the characters involved in each event, as these will go along with the next study, Bible characters.

Major Old Testament Events

- Creation (Gen.1:1-2:3)
- Fall of Man (Gen. 3)
- Flood (Gen. 6-9)
- Babel (Gen. 11:1-9)
- Call of Abraham (Gen. 11:10-12:3)
- Descent Into Egypt (Gen. 46-47)
- Exodus (Ex. 7-12)
- Passover (Ex. 12)
- Giving of the Law (Ex. 19-24)
- Wilderness Wanderings (Num. 13-14)
- Conquest of the Promised Land (Josh. 11)
- Dark Ages of Hebrews (Judges)
- Saul Anointed King (1 Sam. 9:27-10:1)
- Golden Age of Hebrews Under David (United Kingdom) (II Sam. 5:4-5, I Kings 10:6-8)
- Divided Kingdom (I Kings 12:26-33)
- Captivity (II Kings 17-25)
- Return (Ezra)

Major New Testament Events

Early life of Christ
- Ministry of Christ
- Church in Jerusalem
- Church Extending to the Gentiles
- Church Reaching Out to the World

Learning The Bible Through Principle Characters

Many people know some of the Bible characters, but not all. Still others know the characters but can not put them in order. To be able to place the Bible characters in their right setting increases enjoyment of the Bible. String the characters in order from Genesis to Revelation. This will help you "think through" the Bible.

Principle Old Testament Characters

- God
- Satan
- Adam
- Noah
- Abraham
- Isaac
- Jacob
- Joseph
- Pharoah
- Moses
- Aaron
- Caleb
- Joshua
- Othneil
- Deborah
- Barak
- Gideon
- Jephthah
- Samson
- Ruth
- Samuel
- Saul
- David
- Solomon
- Elijah
- Elisha
- Kings of Israel (19)
- Kings of Judah (20)
- Isaiah
- Jeremiah
- Ezekiel
- Daniel
- Nebuchadnezzar
- Cyrus

- Zerubbabel
- Ezra
- Nehemiah
- Esther

Principle New Testament Characters

- John the Baptist
- Jesus Christ
- Disciples of Jesu
- Simon Peter
- James
- John
- Matthew
- Simon
- Philip
- Nathaniel
- Thomas
- James, Son of Alpheus
- Judas, Son of James
- Judas Iscariot
- Stephen
- Philip
- Paul
- James, half-brother of Jesus

Teaching the Bible by Principle Places

You can build your Bible lessons around these places, and you will have the whole story of history in chronological order. As you work through the Bible places, you can review the characters and events. The study of Bible places also lends itself to the study of geography of the Middle East.

Principle Places in the Bible

- Eden
- Mount Ararat
- Babel
- Ur of the Chaldees
- Canaan
- Egypt
- Sinai
- Wilderness
- Canaan
- Assyria
- Babylon
- Canaan (after return of Israelites)

Bible study with children need not be stressful or difficult. You can use this simple framework to customize a curriculum that is just right for your children. My general advice is to do as much enrichment as you are comfortable with. Use these ideas as a guide. (Do not become a slave to your curriculum.)

Good teachers make things simple. They break big chunks of material down into more manageable pieces. Take Granddaddy's framework and hang information on it for your family! By the time you have gone through the *Three Way Bible Learning Process,* you and your children should have a good working knowledge of the sweep of the Scripture.

Make Things Simple

Enrichment Activities

The following activities can be adapted for use in any Bible unit with children.

Bible Information Game

A favorite way to review Bible facts is by playing tic-tac-toe. You can make a board out of anything, but a large poster board works well. Draw the tic-tac-toe lines as usual, making nine squares. Then make five x's and five o's out of construction paper. (Please let children help if they are old enough!)

Write your study questions each day according to what you want to review.

Example: *How many days did it take God to create the world?*
Answer: *6*

After a child answers correctly he or she is allowed to take a turn on the tic-tac-toe board. If you have several children, let them play as teams.

Memorizing

Take sentence strips and write a verse, list of characters, events, or places on them. Cut the words apart and shuffle them. Then allow the children to put the words in order. Variation: Write the words on a small strip of paper, cut words apart and wad up the pieces. Put them in a recycled (empty) prescription pill bottle or other jar with a top and put the lid on. Give children bottles and let them work their own puzzles.

You can also match characters with the place and event.

Hackey Sack Memory Toss

Take a ball or hackey sack and stand in a circle. Let the children throw the ball to each other. Each person catches the ball and says one word of the Bible verse, chronological character list, etc. When somebody misses a word the group has to start over.

Learning the Stories

Let children make up their own play and act it out. Take this as far as you want with video and audio.

Check books out from libraries about Bible characters. Even older children like breezing through picture books that are easy for them.

Learning Events

There is no better way and easier way to put historical events and people in order than the old homeschoolers' stand-by, *the timeline*. These can be done any number of ways. In my day, we homeschooling families displayed our timelines on the walls of our schoolrooms, or even our living rooms! Ready made timelines can be bought as notebooks, but they are very easy to make yourself. You can also string a line across the room and use clothespins to clip the Bible events and characters in order. Children love doing this.

Learning Places

See
Bible
Places

Look in *National Geographic* and *Biblical Archeology Review* magazines and library books for pictures of Bible places. *Google* the names of Bible places for pictures and articles to look at on the computer. Some Bible study software includes pictures of Bible places.

Do map studies on Bible places. A good resource for this is the Bible Atlas published by LifeWay. Make a big map to color while studying the Bible places.

Robin Khoury *is author and publisher of* Answers For New Christians, *a combination storybook, coloring book, workbook and keepsake for elementary children. Contact Robin 405-773-9988 or at littlelightpress@cox.net. Find* Answers For New Christians *as well as other free children's Bible teaching resources at:*

www.answersfornewchristians.com

20
Math

By Penni Hill

Some of our very best memories are of doing elementary age math. When my sons were young, we would do simple math games, and then I would make a worksheet of about ten or fifteen math problems for them. It was a *lot* of fun. For years after, my sons would say, "Remember when *you* did our math, Mom? What a fun time that was."

I approached the subject systematically using Ruth Beechick's books for a guide, building precept upon precept, line upon line. When the time came, my guys tackled long division and multiplied long problems with no difficulties. The transitions were smooth as we moved from one level to the next. Using "hands-on" activities to help cement the concepts in their minds.

There are many ways to teach elementary math with everyday materials, and doing so will help your child to visualize the numbers and operations in their brains. Use concrete materials such as M & M's, balls, Legos, stuffed animals, army guys, etc. to teach addition and subtraction, or have your child count the number of floor tiles in your kitchen. Concepts such as making change, telling time, fractions and measurement can all be taught and once learned, reinforced with "hands on" activities.

Money

To teach money concepts, purchase some play money at a dollar store, then play "store" with your child. If you have lots of change and small bills on hand, use the real stuff. "Sell" books, chairs, paper, pencils, food, and so on. This is fun! Your child will assume you are just playing, when in reality they are learning! I remember buying and selling most of the stuff in my kitchen cabinets. What fun it was for my children to make their purchases. All the while, they were learning to make change and strengthening addition and subtraction concepts that they had learned. They loved it even more when it was my turn to purchase goods. The fun part was writing up a receipt for me!

Time

Teaching time can be done simply by showing your child how to use a clock. Be careful not to push your child ahead too fast. Start by teaching the "on the hour" times, then move onto half hours, and then quarter hours, and finally minute by minute. This process will likely take a few years, depending upon when you start. Please don't expect a four-year-old to understand that "a quarter to four" is the same as 3:45. Children don't understand this fact until they are six or seven, sometimes even older. Remember God made every one of our children an individual, on his or her own learning timetable.

Math

Class

Bakes

Fractions

The next time you are going to bake a cake, have your children join you and help with the preparations. This is a fantastic way to teach fractions as well as liquid measurements. If the recipe calls for three and one-half cups of flour, have them measure this out using different cups. Ask them how many half cups are needed. How many quarter cups? How many three-quarter cups? How about a one-third cup? Can flour in one-third cup measurements go evenly into three and one-half cups?

Show them the measuring spoons, and how many teaspoons go into a tablespoon, and then, how many tablespoons are in one-third cup. When you are finished with "class," you and your children can enjoy dessert together!

Measurement

To teach measurement, simply show your child how to use a ruler. Let them measure in inches, then half inches, and so on. Buy them their own tape measure and ask them to measure their bed, the couch, the table, and their pencil— whatever you can think of! This is learning in action and kids love it! If you don't tell them they won't know this is "school stuff". They will think this is just fun. After all, learning something new is fun and if you can put it to use, it is even more fun!

Internet

Another wonderful resource to help with teaching math is the internet. It can also be a time and money saving resource. Blank practice checks, play money, rulers, practice clocks, and worksheets of nearly every kind can be found for free on the internet. Simply go to your favorite search engine and type in what you want. Type in "blank checks" for instance and you will be directed to websites with a page full of 3 to 4 blank checks to print. Print off several sheets and cut them out. Find and print a ledger page as well. Put these in a small binder or little box. Now your young one can learn how to keep and balance a check-book. Write up utility bills for them. Give them "paychecks". Play store and let them pay with a check. It is a fun activity and one that they will use all their life!

Math Games

Making up your own math games is another way to learn and rein-force math. One of our favorite games we called simply "math on the floor." To play this game all you need is a marker or crayon and some paper! I would generally use approximately twelve sheets of paper, usually the back of letter-size junk mail that. On six sheets I would write simple math equations. On the other six sheets I would write the answers to the equations. Then I would place them on the floor and scramble them up. We would stand on an equation and have to step to the answer. This is also a wonderful method to use when learning to count. Simply write the numbers from one to ten on the papers and have them step in order. Learn math and get some exercise at the same time!

Since we did so many "hands on" activities, we seldom used text-books during the elementary years. We did try different math curricula but none were a good fit for what we needed. So for many years, mostly for ages four through ten, we made our own math worksheets to use for math each day, along with our "hands on" activities. I would write out ten to fifteen problems on a piece of paper, with each problem being written with a different colored marker for variety. It only took me a few minutes and my children loved those papers "Mom used to make." Each page had a few problems for each concept, for example—three addition problems, three subtraction problems, three multiplication problems, and one word problem. After a concept was learned, I would increase the difficulty of the problems. After learning single-digit addition, we moved onto double-digit, then triple-, and so on. With this type of "math curriculum," I always knew exactly where my children were at in math. We could go slowly where there was difficulty, or move faster when more of a challenge was needed.

For more in-depth help with teaching math to elementary age children, I recommend *An Easy Start in Arithmetic* and *You Can Teach Your Child Successfully* by Ruth Beechick. Ruth Beechick's books should be a staple in every home school. She gives age-appropriate teaching guidelines, and explains in detail how to teach the concepts. Another helpful book for this age is *Homeschool Jumpstart Navigator* by Barbara Shelton. Barb Shelton gives a lot of encouragement, tips, and helpful worksheets to use. Also, *Michele's Math* at *www.redshift.com/~bonajo/mmathmenu.htm* has great explanations of how to teach math, step by step. And at Linda Riordan's website *www.bright.net/%7Edouble/math.htm*, Linda tells how she taught her son without using math books. She has posted actual pictures on her site. This site was a great encouragement to me and helped me a lot when my children were younger.

Remember, math does not need to be dull! Be creative when you are teaching math! Include it in your everyday life. If you stop and think about it, you'll realize that you use math all the time. Use these opportunities to teach your child.

- When putting away toys, have your children count them.
- Count how many more cars there are than army guys.
- Have your child set the table, having him figure out how many of each knife, fork and spoon are needed.
- Tell a child to grab a handful of silverware from the drawer and lay them on the table. Then, tell him to figure out how many more are needed.

Teaching preschool and elementary math really can be simple and a whole lot of fun. Make a few fun memories in math class. Years from now, you will be glad you did.

Penni Hill and husband, Nick, have homeschooled their two sons for over thirteen years. In her free time, Penni enjoys making soap, baking bread, reading and doing research. You can learn more about the Hill family at their blog:

www.homesteadblogger.com/trusting/

21
Vocabulary

By Don McCabe

lthough it is important to know that increasing one's vocabulary is beneficial and possible, it is far more important to learn to love words. Through literary learning, your child will encounter many new words and begin to enjoy increasing his vocabulary. He will learn to *love words,* and realize that words—with their power and humor—can be fun. If a person feels affection toward words, he will enjoy learning them. It will be a pleasure. If a person loves words, it won't matter very much what vocabulary-building method is used. They will all work.

Methods

- Some people have developed rather extensive vocabularies very successfully and easily by buying and using many, many cheap—well, comparatively cheap—vocabulary building books.
- Others have managed to accomplish the same thing by keeping little notebooks, into which they jot down every new word that they encounter.
- Still others have acquired a vast word horde by simply reading and making a game out of trying to puzzle out meanings, either before they look them up in a dictionary, or even without looking them up.

When teachers, newscasters, or other adults use some silly academic euphemism, sesquipedalianism, or polysyllabic bit of arcane jargon, a typical response is: "He's just showing off his vocabulary." Rather than admit our ignorance, and our need to learn, we often accuse the other person or writer of knowing too much. Now isn't that silly?

Yet, that is the way I was at one time. When I graduated from high school, I thought I knew everything—at least everything worth knowing. So when I encountered words that I had never seen before, and wouldn't ever see again, I actually thought the writers were showing off. Now, I may still prefer simple, straight-forward writing to the academic, but I have learned that at eighteen I didn't know everything that was worth knowing. Once again, I am learning, and enjoying learning.

Although it seems to be natural to accuse others of showing off when we don't understand them—because it protects us from feeling inferior—it isn't right. We shouldn't feel insulted by the usage of a word we don't know. Instead, we should feel challenged. Here is another opportunity to build our own vocabularies.

Don't we feel challenged when we encounter a new slang word that pops up out of nowhere, but we hear everywhere? We actually signal our "computer" brain to figure out what the word means, and how to use it. We are just "jiving" ourselves if we think we can learn the meaning of "jive" by looking it up in an ordinary dictionary.

Eschew

Obfuscation

Personally, I eschew dictionaries, because I find their definitions to be more obfuscating than helpful But, I have been known to be so mad that I have opened mine, and learned because I wanted to learn.

By the way, remember good writers eschew obfuscation. If a politician says he exchews obfuscation, you know he's using those big words so that nobody will understand exactly where he stands.

Underlining

This desire—this signaling of the brain to learn a word—can be easily accomplished if we read with a pencil. We should underline every word we don't understand. After the fourth or fifth time that we have underlined the same word, one of two things will happen:

1. We will now know the word, because our brain solved the problem for us.
2. We will ask someone what the word means, often angry at ourselves for not having figured it out. Or, we might even use the dictionary!

Reading and Writing

There are other good reasons to get your students in the habit of underlining (or highlighting) words which they don't know while they are reading. The most obvious is that it allows you to find out which words they don't know.

It also leaves a record which can be rewarding both to you and your students when you have them reread from a book with loads of underlined words which they—by then—can read.

As a teacher, I had my students mark up their books with pencil marks instead of copying something and calling it a book report. This way I could tell both how far they had read, and whether or not the book was too easy or too difficult.

- If there are more than five marked words per page, the book may be too difficult.
- Certainly, three underlined words per line (as has happened) indicates the book might as well be written in Sanskrit.
- No underlined words or only one every five or six pages usually indicates the book is too easy.
- In fact, no underlined (or highlighted) words usually means that the student hasn't read the book. Of course, there will always be

those who think they are smarter than the teacher. They will swear up and down that they read all twelve-hundred pages of Tolstoi's *War and Peace,* but they didn't underline or highlight any words because they knew all of them.

Ask them:

1. What's this word?
2. What's this word?
3. What does this word mean?

The answers will reveal if they were bluffing. I tell my students that they must remember the agreement that I made with them:

*They are to read the book and underline in pencil all the words they can't pronounce **and** all words whose meaning they are not sure of, even though they may be able to pronounce them. If they are not willing to do the underlining, then they must do the writing of the five-hundred word book report.*

The real reason for having my students underline or highlight words is to help them discover that they can learn words by themselves—if they alert their brains that there is something that needs to be learned.

The very act of underlining is a cue—a cue to the "computer" brain that there is a problem to solve. Without the cuing by underlining, the pattern of letters skipped over will no more be retained than the *zvcxtwmtqs* of a foreign language, or the position of the telephone poles and fire hydrants you pass by every day on the way to work.

When I tell my students that they may do underlining or write a five-hundred word report, I also give them the reason. I don't want to leave the impression that I'm asking them to underline or highlight because I have stock in a pencil or a highlighter company. I tell them that when they are reading they are bound to come across words they can't pronounce, or whose meaning is beyond them. They can't just stop reading because the word is "lough." They must go on.

Unfortunately, the student doesn't just go on, the student *skips* the word. Skipping is something we do when it isn't important. Skipping words gives the brain the incorrect message.

Underlining gives the correct message. Underlining *cues* the brain that this is a problem for it to solve. If a cue is repeated frequently enough, one of two things is liable to happen. The most common is that the computer brain will solve the problem and all of a sudden you just know what the word is and what the word means. This is how we learned all our basic vocabulary as infants and small children. The computer brain solved problems for us.

The other thing that happens after a specific word is underlined time after time after time, is that even though the computer brain may not have solved the problem it is now triggering you into action. It will try to help you learn by making you mad enough to ask, "Hey Ma, Hey, teacher, Hey anybody, what does lough mean? Does it rhyme with tough, bough, dough, or through?"

I know that constant encountering of the same word can be infuriating, because that's what happened to me when I was reading *Trinity* by Leon Uris. After about the seventh time I encountered that "lough" word that I couldn't pronounce, or even puzzle out the meaning from context (there never was any), I was so furious, I actually used the dictionary. Because I was so angry, I learned that lough is the Irish spelling of lake, and is the same as in Scotland where they spell it loch, but to me sounds like "lock."

Good readers mentally underline words they don't know as they read. Good readers have large vocabularies. This is yet another reason for literature-based learning. However, when beginning to read, it will help your student to mark with a pencil, underline, or highlight words that they don't know.

Underlining is an active process and it helps to make reading an active rather than passive process. To summarize, underlining is valuable because:

- It alerts the brain that the word is a word that needs to be learned.
- It alerts the brain that the particular passage is meaningful to you and you want to remember it.

Don McCabe is research director for AVKO Educational Research Foundation, 3084 W. Willard Road, Clio, MI 48420. Also see Chapter 24, "Spelling," by Mr. McCabe. He may be emailed at avkoemail@aol.com. Phone Toll Free: 866-285-6612 or visit:

www.avko.org

22
Keyboarding

By Leanne Beitel

The first thing students need to learn in keyboarding is technique. They need to learn to sit properly at the computer (or typewriter) and how to press the keys correctly. Discuss with the students that proper technique is necessary for speed and accuracy. When students use proper technique, they are able to type faster, get done faster or even do other things while typing.

Technique

In order to reach all of the keys easily and to type efficiently, there are certain techniques to use:

- Sit up straight and lean in at the waist.
- Keep feet flat on the floor (with one slightly in front of the other for balance).
- Position your body one hand-span (or length) from the keyboard.
- Sit so that the "J" key on the keyboard is opposite your bellybutton.
- Place hands on the homerow (to be introduced in the first lesson).
- Curve fingers.
- Let elbows hang naturally at your side.

- Hold wrists level (not touching the table or the keyboard).
- Keep eyes focused on copy.
- Make sure keyboard is parallel to the table.
- Place text or copy on the right-hand side.
- Use quick, snappy strokes in a rhythmic pace.

After they learn the above, students will then learn how to use the homerow, the spacebar, the punctuation and then the numeric keys. The easiest way for students to learn their keys well is by learning two keys at a time. They will remember when something is repeated, so have them type each letter three times.

Keyboarding Instruction

This will get you started. You can go on to teach the other keys yourself, or use any typing program or software, such as those by Mavis Beacon.

Place your left pinky on the "A." Allow the other fingers to rest on the "S," "D," and "F" keys. Both thumbs will hover over the space bar. Place your right index finger on the "J." Allow the other fingers to rest on the "K," "L," and ";" keys. Most typists use their right thumb to press the space bar.

A. Type the "f" in sets of three, ten times as shown below:

fff fff fff fff fff fff fff fff fff fff

B. Type the "j" in sets of three, ten times as shown below:

jjj jjj jjj jjj jjj jjj jjj jjj jjj jjj

C. Type the "f" and "j" in sets of three, ten times as shown below:

fff jjj fff jjj ffj jjf fjf jfj fff jjj

D. Type the "f" and "j" in sets of three, ten times, pressing "enter" (or "return") with your right pinky at the end of each line as shown below:

fff jjj fff jjj fff jjj fff jjj fff jjj
jjj fff jjj fff jjj fff jjj fff jjj fff
fjf fjf fjf jfj jfj ffj jjf ffj jjf fjf

Speed

After the keys are learned, you can start timing the students for speed and accuracy, using an egg timer, stopwatch or other timing device— or even just by watching the clock, as they type. Your children can copy hymns, song lyrics, the Bible or any text. Start with a one-minute timing. Your student can be given three separate one-minute sessions to attempt improvement. Gradually, work up to five-minute timings, which is the standard for employment testing.

Count words per minute and words with errors. Whether your child has one error in a word, or many errors in a word, it counts as only one error. Net words per minute, then, would be the typed words per minute, less the errors.

If you have more than one child learning how to type, you can create a game where they compete. The one who types the most text with the least amount of errors, while you time the event, wins. Junior high students love this game!

Reports

When your child can type, and has learned how to center his work vertically and horizontally, he can begin doing reports. He can use the spellchecker, word count, and any other tool to help him. For a fun report, have him research his favorite topic and create a report. He may wish to use hyperlinks to related information on the Internet, insert graphics for the cover page, or even add some relevant music.

Scoring is based upon one hundred points. I typically take ten points off per error, when a student is copying the text, since they can just look at the copy and verify that it is accurate (and because a spellchecker is used).

Once you students have mastered reports, they are ready for letters and envelopes. Have your students look at your mail and see the formatting used by insurance companies, utility companies, sales ads, and so on. Discuss the parts of the letter and envelope with them. Have the students compose letters thanking their pastor or Sunday school teacher, or have them type letters requesting information from various colleges. Some students especially liked composing letters to celebrities. You can find celebrity address books in bookstores.

Demonstrate to your students how to write a complaint letter, such as to a television station, using tact and grace. The last type of letter students should learn is the business letter (the most formal letter). Students may first copy (as from an old typing text—sometimes still available from libraries), and then learn how to compose this letter for themselves. Lastly, the envelope can be created using your software, after which your students print the letters and envelopes, and mail.

Proofreader's Marks

Proofreader's marks are what editors (and English teachers) use when checking a writer's work. Find these interesting symbols on the Internet or in old typing or grammar textbooks.

Fun Idea

Using a whiteboard, write a phrase or sentence with errors and then use a different color to mark or edit the incorrect parts. Then have your students rewrite the phrase or sentence correctly.

Next, have the students take turns writing incorrect sentences with proofreader's marks, and another student rewriting the correct sentence. This can be done on paper as well.

Testing

Testing a student's mastery of keyboardng skill should always include technique and timing, as well as a report or letter. An example of a test would be a one-minute timing (watch their technique) and a blank keyboard for the student to fill in. For a more advanced student you could have a five-minute timing, along with an academic report or a business letter.

Leanne Beitel has a masters in secondary training and development, is listed in the Who's Who of American Teachers *and a member of TCEA. She enjoys homeschooling her ten-month old baby girl, Katherine. For further help on keyboarding, contact Leanne at:*

www.christiankeyboarding.com

23

Reviewing

By Wendy Toy

What is reviewing? When the word *review* is broken into its two parts, "view" means *to look at,* while the prefix "re" means *again.* So "to review" is *to look again at the lesson your student has already done.* Of course, in some cases, like with learning math facts, reviewing means you will need to look at the lesson *quite a few more times.*

Reviewing with your student is useful in giving the parent an idea of how much the student remembers from his study, and where a student might need some help. It also gives the student a chance to verbalize some of the facts he has learned, and solidify some of those areas where he may have been a bit unsure. How does this happen?

First, before review can happen, be sure you have covered the lesson in some way. A lesson can consist of reading a book, going on a field trip, watching a tape, listening to a lecture, doing an experiment, visiting a website or even reading a section in a textbook.

Since with reviewing, the student is looking at something again, not hearing it for the first time, be sure that you have covered the subject you want to review, whether you are teaching in a co-op or small homeschool class, or even doing a unit study with a few of your own children. You also need to be aware of any students that may have missed your lesson. They can't review something that they have neither heard nor read before.

Next, decide what your student needs to review.

- Did he come to the end of a chapter in his history book?
- Did he read a biography? —what does he remember from his reading?
- Does she need help in remembering spelling words, math facts, or grammar?

Now create some questions from your student's lesson. To create questions, simply use the five question words you learned when you were in school: *who, what, when, where, why* and *how*. For example:

- *Who was the first postmaster general?* (Benjamin Franklin!)
- *What does a noun name?* (A person, place, thing, idea)
- *When was the Declaration of Independence signed?* (1776)
- *Where is the Statue of Liberty located?* (New York Harbor)
- *Why did George Washington Carver work so much with the peanut?*
- *How many inches are in a foot or feet in a mile?* (You should know this answer!)

Along with knowing the five question words, you need to know that there are various types of questions you can create. These include:

- ***Fill-in-the-blank:*** "The earth _____ around the sun."
- ***Short Answer:*** "Name the nine planets."
- ***Multiple choice:*** "Who was the first president of the United States? *a. Abraham Lincoln, b. John Jay, c.George Washington, d. George Bush*
- ***True or False:*** "A noun always shows action."
- ***Essay:*** "How does the moon get its light?"

After you have created the questions for your review, it's time to select a game to use with your review. Games make it more fun for your student when reviewing.

The steps to adapting a game for review are simple.

1. Be sure to create the review questions you want to use. Although some people like to try to make up questions as they play, writing out the questions is important. This will keep the game flowing and you can be sure that you are covering the material your student needs.

2. Choose a game that has a "pausing point" where you can ask the question. This place should be right before the student takes his turn to spin the spinner, or roll the dice. That way, they will not be able to take their turn unless they answer a question.

3. Go over all the rules of the game before you play. You and your student need to know how to play the game you choose, plus you must decide what will happen if your student answers the question incorrectly. Will he miss a turn? Will the question just go to another student? Will you give the answer and keep the question to ask again later?

Keep in mind that games are only the means to the end (review), the game in this case is not to be a competitive "winner takes all" type of playing. Sometimes a little reward is nice for a job (or review) well done. This could be anything from a food treat to granting a special privilege at your house. Maybe the winner would get a special plate to use at dinner all week, or she could be excused from a chore for one night.

You can use almost any game with review by simply adapting a game you already know how to play. Can you play tic-tac-toe? You can make a tic-tac-toe board on a chalkboard or just on a paper. After you draw the board, ask your student one of your questions. If she gets the answer correct, she gets to put her "x" or "o" on the board. If you have another student also playing, you can ask that student a different question. If he answers correctly, he gets to fill in either the "x" or "o." If you are only reviewing with one student, you can be the other player and take a turn. (You don't have to answer a question if you don't want to!)

Team Review

This game can also be used in small groups. Ask one person on Team "A" the first question and if he is correct, let him write an "x" or "o" in the space of his choice, then ask a question to the first person on Team "B" and let her write an "x" or "o" after a correct answer. Now, ask a question of the second person on Team "A" and continue until everyone gets a turn to answer, and put an "x" or "o" on the board. It ends when one team gets three in a row or when the board is filled. If it ends in a draw, you can play another game or count the number of "x's" or "o's" and see which team has the most.

Another review for a group is to adapt the old familiar "Hot Potato" game. You will need to have your review questions ready, plus you will need a small ball and music that you can turn on and off. Before you begin, always go over the rules of the game so each student will know how to play and what to expect. For this game, you can set a timer to play a certain length of time, or just play until all your review questions have been used. To play as a review game, you will have the students pass the "hot potato" around the circle while the music is playing. At a certain point, after fifteen or twenty seconds, you will turn off the music. The person who is holding the "hot potato" is the one who has to answer a review question. If they get it wrong, they can choose someone else to answer the question. If you decide to have the one who gets the question wrong step outside of the circle, be sure to do it for only one round, then let them back into the game.

Concentration Game

Do you need to review states and their capitals or vocabulary words? You can create a simple concentration review game using three-inch by five-inch cards. Write the state name (or vocabulary word) on one of the cards and the capital or definition on another card. When you have six or seven pairs (or more, depending on the age of your student), turn all the cards over so the writing is face down. Let your student turn over one card and read whatever is on the card. Then she can turn over another card. If the second card is a match with the first card, your student takes both cards and gets to go again. If she misses, she must replace the cards and it is the next person's turn. The game is over when all the cards are turned over, and the winner is the one with the most cards.

Whatever game you choose to play, follow the steps for reviewing and adapting a game, and you can be sure that you are providing a time of both fun and learning in remembering the material that your child has been taught.

Wendy Toy is a fourteen-year homeschooling mom of five boys, and part-time classroom teacher. Her ebook, Creative Review Games, *has tips for review, along with directions, reproducible templates, and patterns that can be used for review games. Visit Wendy's website for many free worksheets for homeschoolers and other helpful ebooks:*

www.toytowntreasures.com

24
Spelling

By Don McCabe

H ere is a vastly different idea for teaching spelling. Students are tested on unknown words, and *not* given the words to study in advance, then, rather than having the teacher correct the test, each student corrects each word as the test is given. This *sequential spelling technique* is based on the concept that the natural way of learning is by making mistakes, in which immediate self-correction takes place. This is the way we learned to walk, talk, read (see other chapter by Mr. McCabe), feed ourselves and ride a bike.

The reasoning behind this technique is that if a student misses an easy word he has studied, he will learn the wrong thing—that he is dumb. However, if a student misses something that was never assigned, it's to be expected. Moreover, if a student gets a word (that he has not studied) correct, then he's smart!

Using this technique, I was able—in a class composed of twenty-five juvenile delinquents with reading levels initially ranging from grade one to grade eight—to get every single student to spell correctly and read the word "installment."

Word Families

It is best to test on realated words. Words within "families" have similar letter combinations, such as the "ai" in main, sail and pair. These patterns make it easier for the student to learn from previous mistakes, and also to to acquire a more challenging vocabulary. For example, even in the very simple "at" family, there is the word scat, and scatting which has a special meaning to jazz enthusiasts, or tatting which is a special way of making lace. These word families make it much easier for students to immediately apply what they learn from one word to another. This is sometimes called "vertical word processing." For example:

> **all**
> t**all**
> st**all**
> inst**all**
> inst**all**ment
> inst**all**ation

You can construct your own word-family lists, or you can search the Internet using as keywords, "spelling, word, family, lists." Or see: ***www.enchantedlearning.com/rhymes/wordfamilies/***

To build your own lists, all you have to do is run through the possible consonants such as "b," "c," "d," "f," "g," etc. and put them in front of the common letters, "ai." *Bain* and *dain* are not words, but *Cain* and *gain* are. After you finish with single consonants, put the blends in front of "ain" such "br," "cr," "gr," "tr," "str," etc. and see which make real words. Then check the digraphs such as "ch," "sh," "th," and "wh."

In this case, only "ch" + "ain" make a real word. Just try adding letters in front of the ending and keep the real words that you want to use.

After you have found three word families that need to be mastered, make out your list of words that belong to each word family. Then, test your students' ability to spell the ending sounds of words by giving them the onsets (initial letters, consonants, digraphs, blends). Tests can be varied in length from five to twenty-five words according to your students' needs, enthusiasm, and time available. For example:

pain
*The first letter in **pain** is "p." Spell **pain**, as in, "Correcting papers is a **pain** in the neck."*

sail
*The first letter in **sail** is "s." Spell **sail**, as in, "to sail a boat on a lake."*

chair
*The first two letters in **chair** are "ch." Spell **chair** as in, "to sit in your **chair**."*

Sequential Spelling Test

- *Give the word. Repeat the word. Use the word in a sentence.* You may write the sentences on worksheets with blanks to fill in with the spelling word. (More on this later.)

- *Have students repeat the word, or word and sentence.* With older students this step may be eliminated.

- *Have students attempt the spelling.* It is essential that each student at least makes an attempt. In order to learn from a mistake, a mistake must be made. In order to learn to tolerate personal mistakes, mistakes must be made in an atmosphere that allows for mistakes.

- *Show the correct spelling on an overhead projector or on a chalkboard or whiteboard.*

- *Call out the word and the letters. Each student repeats the word and the letters, and corrects his or her own spelling.* If a mistake has been made, the student is to erase the incorrect spelling before writing the word correctly. *The students must never make a check mark.* No matter how many words a student may miss during the test, the paper should look exactly the same as that of a student who correctly spelled every word the first time.

- *Repeat steps one through five for each word.*

- Teacher gives word
- Students repeat word
- Students write word
- Teacher gives correct spelling
- Students correct own spelling before next word is given

Pace is essential. The greatest music is boring if it is dragged out. Speed and liveliness of presentation is vital.

No Prior Study

Remember, do *not* give the words to the students to study. When students study words for a test and then miss them, they only learn to believe that they are dumb! Students don't feel dumb if they miss a word they weren't given for study—but if they get one right that they know they didn't know the day before —*wow!* They know they have to have some "smarts" after all.

Note from Lorraine: This builds their self-esteem and will multiply results in all learning.

Dictation Technique

Not all words fit into families. To work on the irregular words I would dictate sentences. To do this, I dictated two sentences (and two sentences only) each day for about a month. For example: For three days, the emphasis might be on: "quit," "quite," and "quiet." On one day the two sentences might be:

Dictate Two Sentences

- *If you're **quiet,** we might **quit quite** soon.*
- *Does your mother know that you're planning to **quit** your job?*

On another day, the two sentences might be:

- *Does your **principal** know what courses you're planning to take?*
- *If you're going to your **principal's** office, don't tell him that he doesn't have any **principles.***

This technique worked well, except for those few students who could hardly spell their own names. A sentence like either of the second ones above was far too long. In this case, I individualized.

Individualizing

For challenging students, I devised three levels of difficulty for the same sentence, such as the following:

- *You are doing **quite** nicely, but I wish you would **quit** being so **quiet.***

I first typed out the correctly spelled sentences as above. Then, I used Liquid Paper to "erase" just what I wanted these students to concentrate their energies on. Their sentence would look like this:

• _ou are doing qu____ nicely, but I wish _ou would qu__ being so qu____ .

The average students would have the same sentence, except that I would have more of it whited out.

• ____ ____ doing _____ nicely, but I wish ____ _____ _____ being so _____.

The best students would have the same sentence, but would have to write the entire sentence with no help.

By reading the sentence together, the "slower" students were able to pick up a great many reading skills as well as spelling skills.

For variety, you may elect to mix up the endings so that the students will have to be alert and not just automatically add the "s" or the "ed" or the "ing" as the case may be. For example, one day's words might include *rain, trains, strained,* etc., and the next day's might be *rains, train, straining,* etc.

Sequential spelling is a method that works. It's simple and it follows solid principles of learning. However, there may be times in which the word family being presented has already been learned by your students. We feel that this isn't necessarily bad. Overlearning is right for many.

Sequential
Spelling
Works

Don McCabe has advanced degrees in English literature, psychology, philosophy, and reading, with minors in history and theology. Write to the AVKO Foundation Spelling Division, 3084 W. Willard Road, Clio, Mich., 48420, for a free spelling catalog. For more information about the sequential spelling technique or any other topic related to reading, writing, and spelling, visit:

www.spelling.org

25

Literature for Teens

By Janice Campbell

G reat books are special. They capture the heart and mind of readers, century after century. Great books enlarge thinking, expand the known world, and bring abstract concepts such as justice, love and truth to life. It's really impossible to be literate, in the classic sense, without being well-read, for reading is the foundation of literacy.

Choosing the Best

How can you choose the great books that will form the heart of your high school literature curriculum? As you look out on the array of available options, it can be daunting to think of narrowing the field to the very best. Yet that is what you'll have to do.

To help with this challenging task, you may want to find a mentor who is well-versed in the classics and can offer guidance, or you might prefer to select a curriculum that's compatible with your goals. You may even decide to do what I did, and return to college to study literature, so that you'll be able to choose wisely for yourself! As you probably won't have time for the last option, I'll share my personal list of "must-read" books for teens.

Since there is so much wonderful literature available, I suggest starting the serious study of great works in the eighth grade. This allows two years to explore a variety of literature before jumping into the more complex works. We read novels, short stories, poetry, essays and drama, and in that way, students become acquainted with some of the less intimidating great works. The next three years are spent differently. I recommend that all students do a chronological survey of American Literature and British Literature, followed by a year of World Literature. Here is the sequence I suggest:

English I, Introduction to Literature

Short Stories by:
- Guy De Maupassant
- O'Henry
- Edgar Allen Poe
- James Thurber
- Eudora Welty

Novels:
- *A Connecticut Yankee in King Arthur's Court* by Mark Twain
- *Charlotte Bronte* by Jane Eyre
- *Pygmalion* by George B. Shaw
- *Robinson Crusoe* by Daniel Defoe
- *Animal Farm* by George Orwell
- "A Modest Proposal" by Johnathan Swift

Year 2, Literature and Composition

- *Walden* by Henry D. Thoreau
- *The Three Musketeers* by Alexandre Dumas
- *The Screwtape Letters, 'Til We Have Faces* by C.S. Lewis
- *My Antonia* by Willa Cather
- *The Importance of Being Ernest* by Oscar Wilde
- *Heart of Darkness* by Joseph Conrad
- *Around the World in Eighty Days* by Jules Verne
- *The Lord of the Rings* by J.R. R. Tolkein

Year 3, Chronological Survey of American Literature

- Colonial Period—*The Autobiography of Benjamin Franklin*
- Age of Romanticism—Whitman, Poe, Emerson, Hawthorne, Melville, Dickinson
- Age of Realism—*Huckleberry Finn* by Mark Twain, *Portrait of a Lady* by Henry James
- Age of Naturalism—*House of Mirth* by Edith Wharton
- Modernism—*The Great Gatsby* by F. Scott Fitzgerald; *A Moveable Feast, Old Man and the Sea* by Ernest Hemingway

Year 4, Chronological Survey of British Literature

- Middle English—*Canterbury Tales* by Geoffrey Chaucer; *Sir Gawain and the Green Knight*
- Jacobean Age—*King Lear* by William Shakespeare
- 17th-18th Century—*Paradise Lost* by John Milton
- Romantic Movement—*Pride and Prejudice* by Jane Austen
- Victorian Age—*Oliver Twist* by Charles Dickens; *Wuthering Heights* by Emily Bronte
- Modernism—*To the Lighthouse* by Virginia Woolf

Year 5, Geographical Survey of World Literature

- Greece—*The Odyssey* by Homer; *Antigone* by Sophocles
- Middle East—Bible, "Job"
- Italy—*Aeneid* by Virgil; *Inferno* by Dante Alighieri
- Spain—*Don Quixote* by Miguel de Cervantes
- France—*Les Miserables* by Victor Hugo
- Russia—*Crime and Punishment* by Fyodor Dostoevsky
- Germany—*Faust* by Wolfgang Goethe

How to Study the Great Books

And how should your student study literature? According to Charlotte Mason, in *School Education,* the essential thing is to allow your student to learn directly from the great books. She states:

> *I think we owe it to* [the students] *to let them dig their knowledge, of whatever subject, for themselves out of the fit book; and this for two reasons: What a child digs for is his own possession; what is poured into his ear, like the idle song of a pleasant singer, floats out as lightly as it came in, and is rarely assimilated. I do not mean to say that the lecture and the oral lesson are without their uses; but these uses are, to give impulse and to order knowledge; and not to convey knowledge, or to afford us that part of our education which comes of fit knowledge, fitly given. . . . Ideas must reach us directly from the mind of the thinker, and it is chiefly by means of the books they have written that we get into touch with the best minds.*

The heart of literature study is the book itself. In order for the student to get the most benefit and joy from the reading, it's important to set the stage for it by providing context information. If your teen has read a bit about the author and the historical period in which the book was written, he or she will have a much greater understanding and enjoyment when reading the book. For the most challenging works, such as Chaucer's *Canterbury Tales* or Milton's *Paradise Lost,* I recommend reading an overview or synopsis before diving into the text. It's much easier to understand epic poetry or Middle English when you have some idea of what's going on!

Provide

Context

Info

For each work of literature you assign, I suggest the following study sequence for teens:

1. Read brief context information about the author and the historical time in which the book was written.

2. If possible, listen to a bit of music that the author may have listened to, read at least one poem of the period, and look at an art history book or online to see what sort of art was being created at the time the book was written.

3. For the most challenging books, read a brief synopsis of the work, such as you find in *SparkNotes* or *CliffNotes*. This is not necessary for most works, but I recommend it for those with archaic language, and for epic poetry. Although many people associate study guides—such as those I just mentioned—with cheating, these guides are simply intended to help the student understand a work, just as a parent or teacher would do. It is only when the guide is read *instead* of the book that the use constitutes cheating!

4. Read the work all the way through, at a comfortable pace. Read fast enough to sustain interest, but slowly enough to understand what is happening. Focus on enjoying the story!

5. As you read, keep a piece of paper tucked into the back of the book. Write down any words you encounter that you don't know, and look them up later. (Also see Mr. McCabe's underlining suggestion in Chapter 21.) If you're reading a book with a lot of characters, you may want to make a list so you can keep them straight. And finally, write down interesting insights that occur to you, as well as quotes that seem significant. All this will be helpful to you as you write your essay.

6. When you've read the book, write an approach paper for it. The approach paper should include a brief summary, character analysis, discussion questions, key passage, and an explanation of the

key passage. This will help you think through the book, and prepare you for writing the essay.

7. Write the essay, answering a very specific essay question. These may be found in study guides.

Francis Bacon once suggested that "some books are to be tasted, others to be swallowed, and some few to be chewed and digested." The great classics are worthy of being chewed and digested, so I suggest taking time to appreciate them, perhaps allowing four weeks for each assignment sequence. By the time this sequence is completed for each chosen book, the student should have a deep understanding of the work, and often, a love for great literature.

Whether your teen follows a self-directed course, or you choose to make literature a family affair, you'll find that reading, studying and talking about the great books can enrich your family's life. As Alexander Solzhenitsyn reminds us,

> *The sole substitute for an experience which we have not ourselves lived through is art and literature . . . . Literature transmits incontrovertible condensed experience . . . from generation to generation. In this way, literature becomes the memory of a nation.*

Literature
Creates
Legacy

When your teen discovers and shares an unforgettable book with the family, literature—and the experience that it contains—becomes part of your family's memories. What a valuable legacy!

Janice Campbell is an alternative education specialist, writer, speaker, and author of *Transcripts Made Easy, Get a Jump Start on College!* and the *Zeitgeist Literature* series, which includes suitable specific essay questions for your student's literature studies. For resources to help you homeschool through high school and beyond, see:

www.EverydayEducation.com

26
Lapbooking

By Cyndi Kinney, R.N.

By incorporating lapbooks, notebooking pages, and copywork notebooks you can add variety to your literature studies. Are the terms "lapbook," "notebooking," and "copywork" foreign to you? Perhaps you have heard of them and think they take too much preparation and time. Maybe you think your kids are too old, or too young, to benefit from these teaching techniques. Maybe you already have a curriculum set up within your homeschool and you "don't want to add anything else." All of these concerns are valid. However, once you see the benefits of these tools and how easy it can be to incorporate them, you will see that you can't afford *not* to give them a try.

Lapbooking

What is a lapbook? Remember the old-style "pop-up" books that you had when you were a child? Well, lapbooks are similar. Technically, a lapbook is nothing more than some folders and paper booklets, arranged and folded in unique ways. But oh, it is really *so* much more than that!

A lapbook is an enjoyable technique for displaying a summary of what a student has learned and accomplished during a particular unit of study. It may include maps, vocabulary, creative writing, coloring, drawings, questions and answers, reports and much more. One of the most amazing things about lapbooks is that they can be created for *any* subject and at *any* age or grade level. Lapbooks also teach your students to become good "detectives" and researchers.

So, I can hear you saying, "Sounds like a lot of paper and glue to me. Why should I bother?" Well, I'm glad you asked! Lapbooking helps to improve retention of materials learned, and reinforces topics. Lapbooks can motivate creative students and help "creatively-challenged" students to accomplish tasks in exciting ways. Lapbooking also sparks reluctant writers and budding artists. It allows for a "fun" way of studying an otherwise challenging topic and reinforces the connection between writing and reading.

Lapbooks can replace testing, as they display what was learned. They can also be used as an evaluation tool. On this same note, they can show family members a "bird's eye view" of what the student has learned about a particular topic. I have seen my daughter's eyes light up when she has shown her lapbooks to people. She is even surprised, herself, by how much she remembers from the studies where she used lapbooks!

Studies show that children retain more information when they use more of their senses in the learning process. Lapbooking involves brightly colored shapes (sight) that the children fold and place into the folders (touch). The student can record voice, reciting something from the study, or telling what has been learned, and place this recording on a disc that slips into a pocket inside the lapbook (hearing).

The students are encouraged to document recipes, trying recipes from the era or country they are studying (taste). And last, but not least, there are "scratch-n-sniff" booklets (smell)! That's all five senses, so you can plan on a *lot* of information retention with a lapbook!

Use The Senses

The Lapbook Base

So, how do you get started? All you need is two or three file folders. I am going to explain the process, assuming that you are using two file folders for your lapbook.

1. Open up one of the file folders in front of you.

2. Leave the "tabs" on the file folder because it gives you a little extra room for booklets later on.

3. Start on the left side of your opened file folder, and fold that side so that the edge (or tab) touches the center crease of the folder. (If your folder has four center creases, first score a line with a metal ruler and ballpoint pen, exactly in the center of those four creases and then make a new crease.) After folding the edge in to the center, you will have a "flap" that is just as tall as the original folder and half as wide. Make a really good crease along the portion that you have just folded. Let's call this new fold that you have made on the left side of the folder "A." You may wish to mark it "A" with a pencil, so you can later erase.

4. Now, do the same thing on the right side of the file folder, again making sure to make a really good crease in your new fold. Let's call the fold you have made on the right side "B."

5. Now, put this folder aside, and take out the second folder.

6. Do the exact same steps (2, 3 and 4) for this file folder, but call the fold that you make on the left "C," and the fold that you make on the right "D."

7. Now, you have two file folders, each with two folded "flaps" that "stick up" a little. We will call the sides of the flaps that are facing up "Side 1" and the sides of the flaps that are facing down toward the rest of the folder "Side 2."

8. Place *both* file folders in front of you, with the flaps on top. The first folder that you prepared (with flaps "A" and "B") should be on your left, and the second file folder that you prepared (with flaps "C" and "D") should be on your right.

9. Now, put several lines of glue on "Side 1" of flap "B."

10. Place "Side 1" of flap "B" (with the glue on it) against "Side 1" of flap "C" so that now your file folders are attached to each other. (If you want the file folder tabs to line up perfectly, then you may have to turn one of the folders around, but it really isn't necessary for the tabs to line up.) Just make sure that you keep the folders facing up, where the "flaps" stay on top. You may also want to put a few staples in this attached area, to secure a little better.

11. Now you have one large folder, with a flap on each end and in the middle. If you have followed the directions correctly, your project will (when lying on the table in front of you) now have flaps "A" and "D" on the ends, and flaps "B" and "C" in the middle (connected by the glue), with all flaps on the SAME side of the project (pointing up, if you will). This is called your *lapbook base*.

12. You will glue fifteen to twenty small booklets randomly inside this lapbook base. There is no "correct" way to arrange the booklets, unless you have a certain reason for keeping them in order, based on your theme of study. Each booklet (or "mini-book") will be different from the others, depending on your imagination and subject matter. The booklets are usually anywhere from one inch to five inches in size. You will want to keep them from being too large, unless you have a certain topic that is really important, and you may then decide to have one really large booklet along with sev-

eral small ones. You may want to start with just blank paper, folding it over like a card. Write the name of a person or event on the outside and then have the student write about it further on the inside. A great way to start is by created "shape booklets," cutting geometric shapes (two of the same size) and stapling them together. Use your imagination and create "house-shaped" booklets for describing someone's home, "animal-shaped" booklets for describing pets, "train-shaped" booklets to describe transportation, and so on. You may also glue maps and worksheets within the lapbook base or within a booklet, if you like. Search the Internet for "shape-book" templates and other types of folded booklets. Have your kids cut booklets in shapes that con-

nect, like triangles, rectangles, circles, octagons. Geometric shapes are always fun for creating booklets! You can even cut out booklets that are in the shapes of the characters or their homes, or even their pets, or you might start simply with folding paper over like a greeting card and get more creative later.

13. To close the Lapbook, start on the right side of your Lapbook Base, and fold flap "D" back in toward the original crease in the folder. (You will not have to make any creases, just fold along the lines that you made in steps three through six). Now, fold flap "A" in the same manner. Now, fold the entire Lapbook together, like a book. All flaps will be inside the lapbook base.

14. The outside of the lapbook can be decorated in many ways, depending on your unit of study. Draw pictures, glue pictures, or use paint to decorate it.

Learning with the Lapbook

For a literature-based lapbook, create different booklets for plot, characters, setting, climax, summaries, conflicts, symbolism, vocabulary, predictions, and other literary elements within the text of the book. This can get really exciting! Enjoy drawing, researching, comparing and contrasting characters and settings. In all subjects, as you come to something interesting, create a small booklet about it. Inside the booklet, you may choose to have your child draw a picture, write a story, or just glue pictures. Students can write a question on the outside of the booklet and answer it on the inside. The possibilities are endless!!

Copywork

Copywork is a great way to teach your children about literature and history. By copying passages from classics or historical documents, children learn many areas of the language arts. Children have the opportunity to be exposed to great writers and facts, while learning spelling, punctuation, grammar, vocabulary, and creative writing from the "Masters." Most classical education programs recommend copywork as an integral part of educating children, and many actually use copywork in place of traditional language arts programs.

By copying passages two to three days per week (or more), your children will come to learn and possibly memorize some of the greatest literature from our history. While penmanship is important, the knowledge gained through the copywork is what is most important.

However, do encourage your children to take pride in their penmanship. Also, instruct them in the importance of the art of spelling, punctuation, grammar, vocabulary and creative writing. With some practice, they will begin to imitate the masters in their own personal writing.

The amount of recall of spelling and punctuation rules will amaze you! My daughter always had trouble in these areas, until we started copywork! Wow, what a difference! In addition, I have found my daughter using words in her vocabulary and writing that I didn't know she knew!

Notebooking

Notebooking is a great way to preserve your child's work. Notebooking allows a child to have fun, while creatively journaling and documenting learning. Some families create and keep notebooks for every subject. Others only keep notebooks for specific topics such as unit studies, history or science. Following your child's cues, allow him to use notebooking for subjects that he is truly passionate about!

You may choose to use a three-ring binder for your notebook, and place each completed page in a sheet protector for extra protection.

Remember to let your child follow his or her imagination. Let him draw pictures (or cut and glue them) on the pages. Allow him to make many copies of the same page if he really likes that page. Let him make pages of his own! Encourage individuality, and assure your child that there is no right or wrong way to "do notebooking." That is the true beauty of notebooking! Allow your child to take ownership and to create a notebook that is uniquely his.

Notebooking Supplies

- *Notebooks:* The best ones (in my opinion) are the ones that allow you to add your own artwork behind the clear cover.
- *Scissors:* You will want regular scissors as well as paper edger scissors for cutting out clip art, trimming the edges of papers and other activities.
- *Pens and pencils:* Make sure you have nice pens and colored or fancy pencils available.

- **Glue:** Purchase glue sticks, rubber cement and tape.
- **Stickers:** Scrapbooking stickers are great for notebooks! We also like to use sticker markers to create our own stickers! We also like using sticker letters to create titles.
- **Stampers:** If you enjoy stamping, rubber stamps can be lots of fun in notebooks. Be sure to buy washable ink, or you may be sorry!
- **Clip Art:** You can get great clip art from the Internet, and most is free to use, if it is used for educational purposes at home.

Be Creative

The best thing about notebooking is that you can be creative. Have fun with lapbooking, copywork and notebooking! Let your classes go from boring to *boing!*

Cyndi Kinney, R.N. has created a business out of making lapbooks and teaching people how to use them. Knowledge Box Central designs lapbooks for Tapestry of Grace, and learning products for Jeannie Fulbright and for Apologia's Elementary Science Series. For help or inspiration, visit:

www.knowledgeboxcentral.com

27

Computer

By Susie Glennan

eing creative is so important for home school parents. If you have a hard time being creative, then learn how to research online and offline to find what you need when you need it. But try not to be on the computer so much that it cuts into your school and family time.

As my children were growing up in a home school environment, I was blessed to have an uncle who worked for a major tech company and a husband who was great at doing research. My husband used to plan field trips with my uncle in the San Francisco Bay area to help with the children's hands-on learning. Because of this we have been to the Intel® Museum, Exploratorium, Tech Museum, and everything else we could find in the San Francisco Bay area.

At one of our many trips to the Intel® Museum, we learned about educational materials and tools Intel® offers to those in the education profession (*www.intel.com/education/tools/*). One of them was *The Journey Inside*[SM] (*www.intel.com/education/journey/index.htm*). I sent away for the kit and was able to teach a group of children about the workings of a computer. I'm sure Intel® has updated things since I taught this curriculum. You should definitely check out their website and education offerings.

When the package arrived, I studied how to teach different grade levels, as I would be teaching several children who signed up for the class. Then I made a shopping list of things I thought would enhance the curriculum. Next I prepared each student's lesson. This is such a great program that the only other things I thought would help add to the curriculum were a different motherboard, individual components from computers that were no longer in use, aluminum foil, sand and a few other things that went with the supplemental lesson ideas.

We started with the kids talking about what they thought a computer was, and did. Then we let them talk about what they do on their own computers and what we would learn about computers. Next we popped in the video that came with the curriculum. The visuals were great. In order to meet the needs of all of the children in my class I felt I needed to reach out to as many of their senses as possible. This program does just that. It allows them to watch a movie, read the information, fill in blanks (write), talk about what they see and work on activities (touch).

Each class was an exciting time for the kids to learn and explore. Most often they'd come in with a story of how they used their computer, or show off a new puzzle they came up with by using binary code. Some of the parents would sit in because it was so fun.

In the beginning we went over history of where computers came

from. We also had physical hardware components from computers that were no longer needed, to show everyone what the inside of the computer looked like. The kids held a motherboard in hand and we pointed to where the information path was. It started in one chip and moved throughout the board. We explained what all of the different parts of the computer were, and what they did. Then we moved on to how the information was processed using 0's and 1's.

We also went over the different types of memory. I was able to come up with analogies to help the kids understand better. I would give the name, acronym, and definition from the dictionary, then my analogy.

Random Access Memory: RAM—*the most common computer memory which can be used by programs to perform necessary tasks while the computer is on; an integrated circuit memory chip allows information to be stored or accessed in any order and all storage locations are equally accessible.*

Analogy: When you're using a computer, it has only so much RAM. While you may have a lot of space on your actual hard drive, the RAM is what processes the information of the programs that are open and in use. If you open up too many programs, your computer will tell you that there isn't enough memory to open up that program. You must first close some of the things you are working on to free up RAM.

Free

Some

Space

It's the same with your brain. When you have too much information on the desktop of your brain, you might have trouble bringing more information to the forefront unless you free up some space. Therefore, you should write down some of that information to release it from your thoughts, freeing up space to work on the next project or issue.

Read Only Memory: ROM—*computer memory in which program instructions, operating procedures, or other data are permanently stored, generally on electronic chips during manufacture, and that ordinarily cannot be changed by the user.*

Analogy: When a book is published, the text is there for good. In order to change the text in a book, you must do a reprint. It's the same with the memory on your computer called ROM. If you want to change the instructions on the computer you'll have to build a new one with a new motherboard.

There are forty-three chapters in *The Journey Inside*[SM], so I'll stop here and let you have the fun of starting at the beginning and coming up with creative ways to go all the way through to the end.

Because we were open to new ideas and different ways of teaching as the Lord provided, we were able to give the children a fulfilling homeschool experience. When we first started telling others in our homeschool group about the computer curriculum, many parents (and their children) became interested in learning along with us. We knew this was going to be an important field of learning, and apparently others did, too. Thus, this became a main focus of study during 1993 and 1994.

Susie Glennan has been happily married since 1982, has four children and two grandchildren. Susie homeschooled for eight years. She teaches seminars on various topics and is the president of The Busy Woman, Inc. See Susie's site:

www.thebusywoman.com

28

Organization

By Susie Glennan

very time I embarked on one of my journeys of teaching a new curriculum, I'd compartmentalize everything needed in order to keep it all in one place. For example, the unit of study described above was all about computers and electronics. So we had a section of shelves in our teaching room just for the components of this study.

Let's talk about compartmentalizing for a moment. When you compartmentalize your home, homeschool, car, work, etc., you delegate a place for like items. It's the same as categorizing. This allows you to keep track of what you have, and gives you easy access to each category of items when needed.

In our homeschool, each child had their own file box with schoolbooks inside. We used cardboard for dividers with the subject at the top of each divider. So whether the kids were going to be in the car or at the table, their work was organized in such a way, they knew where everything was. When the kids were very young, I had all curriculum organized for my learning and personality styles. As the kids grew older I transferred the responsibility to them by helping them set up their own organization according to their own learning and personality styles. For everyone as a group, there was a drop off and pick up tray, a schedule and a mini office supply store in one area, separated in different drawers.

It took us about three weeks to arrange the house in an orderly fashion, making a place for everything. When we were done, we had a picnic in the backyard to celebrate. I found it important to show them how much "FREE TIME/Me Time©" we had, after school and chores were completed. It was all clearly defined and marked on the schedule until it became routine. After the schedule became a routine, we only had to write on the schedule the basics because everyone knew that two o'clock was time to clean up and do chores.

I also taught the children about time increments. When a specific time for chores was over, we stopped what we were doing and moved on. Sometimes that meant leaving things incomplete or chores undone. This taught them about time limits. When you dawdle, things do not get completed. This life lesson has transferred into their young adult lives. I can finally see the results of my labor.

Some moms would say that we were "too" organized and they don't want to have to live that way. I'm living proof that all it did was give us more time to enjoy. It also gave us more flexibility for sick days, field trips, or a day just to be lazy and take a break. Because we all knew what was expected of us, and lived in an orderly way, we could be flexible when plans had to change. It also trained our children for later life as they move out on their own.

As far as curriculum compartmentalizing, it made it so much easier to see what materials we had available for each subject. At one glance we could see all that we had for *The Journey Inside* curriculum, which made it easier for me to buy what we didn't have. Was there ever a time you were out of the house and saw something that you thought would be such a great addition to your curriculum that you purchased it only to find out when you got home that there was one of those or something similar buried at the bottom of a box?

Having an orderly home environment does not make you a slave to your home. It honestly frees up valuable time. I've lived both extremes and can tell you that I'd rather be over-organized than under-organized.

God speaks of organization throughout the Bible. I'll leave you with these verses: *For God is not a God of disorder but of peace. But everything should be done in a fitting and orderly way.* (1 Cor. 14:33, 40) Now God, of course, is talking about orderly worship in these two verses. However, He wants us to have an orderly, and therefore, peaceful life as well.

Susie Glennan teaches others to use their God-given personalities to enhance their lives and relationships—through effectively managing their time and staying true to the values in life that are most important to them. For daily planners, purses, car and home organizers, memory books and other organizing tools to help enhance the busy life of today's family, go to:

www.thebusywoman.com

29

Life Curriculum

By Marilyn Rockett

While growing up, I thought a house magically cleaned itself. My mother had a full-time housekeeper—in those days, we called them maids—who cleaned while I was at school. I didn't see anyone mop a floor, clean a toilet, strip bed linens, sort laundry, or clean out a refrigerator (a job I still dislike). I lived a "Cinderella" life, but I was always at the ball. I laughingly say now that it probably would have done me good to have a wicked stepmother making me work.

While I'm not advocating that you morph into a wicked witch while requiring your children to help around the house, I *am* saying that neglecting that responsibility will encumber their adult lives in ways you may not realize. Conversely, teaching your children to work properly will produce many life advantages. They gain a stronger work ethic, a sense of teamwork with others, a servant heart, self-confidence in knowing how to do everyday tasks, a realization that they must complete jobs they start, and the awareness that the world doesn't revolve solely around their desires. Wouldn't you want to know a person like that? Wouldn't an employer want an employee like that? Wouldn't an entrepreneur possess those qualities?

Motherhood is not for wimps! The task of raising children, teaching them life skills, instilling proper work habits, and homeschooling them is a serious commitment of paramount importance that presents many challenges. You want your children to learn math, science, grammar, reading and many more subjects that are essential. Nevertheless, it's easy to overlook foundations in the rush to cover academics.

Your persistent effort in training can reap regular rewards for you, for your family, and for your children. Using a LIFE curriculum accomplishes the job best: Lead. Instruct. Facilitate. Encourage.

Lead

The most effective teachers lead by example. Your children learn best the things you model for them. It is possible that you weren't taught how to run a household well. I wasn't, and it is a challenge to have to learn to do a good job, later in life. Maybe you have the wrong attitude about your homekeeping, thinking it isn't very important as long as the kids learn their math. You may feel that children should be children as long as they can; consequently, you don't require them to help around the house. You may think that household work is trivial and not important to your children's character development—it is just work that has to be done for your family to survive. If you are a perfectionist, you may prefer to do it yourself rather than hassle with the children about doing chores. On the other hand, do you expect your children to clean their bedrooms when yours is a mess? Must they pick up their possessions and put them away when your belongings are scattered throughout the house? You get the idea. Sorry to step on toes—I'm trying to do it gently—but there is no way around the fact that your children follow your lead as you model attitudes and actions.

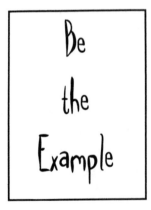

Whatever reason you have for neglecting to teach life skills to your children, this neglect will show in your children's attitudes, their work ethic and even in their academics.

Instruct

While leading by example is important, even if you keep a perfect home, your children will not know what to do or how to do it if they don't participate in the process. If you clean while they play outside or while they sleep, they will think, as I did, that there is a "cleaning fairy godmother" while they attend the ball.

I can assure you that your definition of "clean your room" and your children's definitions are not the same. Define it for them by showing them your measure of a clean room. You must give them clear instructions and expectations of the jobs you're asking them to do. Be specific. Show them how and allow them to do the job while you watch.

In each room that your children clean and straighten, post a checklist of the tasks you consider necessary before the room earns your "clean" approval. Room checklists work better than a central chore chart, because the standard is readily available for reference without your child making a trip to a central chart in the kitchen. A child, on the way to another room to check the list, will be far too easily distracted!

Facilitate

You are not just cleaning your house but training your children for the future. They need your help to learn well. Be available for them, letting them know they should come to you with questions or difficulties.

If a child is having trouble doing a certain chore, examine why. Is the chore too difficult for his age and ability? Has he misunderstood how to do the chore? Does the child have a bad attitude, making the chore difficult in his or her mind? Yes, there are children who whine and complain, but you train them best by helping, without doing the job for them. Some children learn quickly that when they whine,

Momma will bail them out by doing the chore, or she will ignore the unfinished chore to keep from hearing the complaints.

Work with your children rather than doing other tasks while they clean. When the entire family works together, even at different jobs or in different rooms, your children have a sense of teamwork motivating them to accomplish a task. Try setting a certain time of day and length of time for everyone to work.

Make work fun as you are able, but don't try to make a game out of everything they do, creating the impression that everything in life has to be "fun." Play music while you all work. Laugh. For some children, and often with boys, creating a challenge motivates them. Set a timer to see if they can finish a task before the time is up, or challenge them to finish their chore before you finish your chore.

Offer incentives on occasion—a trip to the park when you finish working, a special treat or snack after the hard work, or a coupon to redeem for something special. Offer these treats as a surprise at random times rather than as rewards each time they work. As adults, they won't receive a reward every time they are required to do a job, so they shouldn't expect those things while they are young. Avoid the temptation to reward good behavior by allowing them to skip their chores or to punish bad behavior by making them do extra chores. That may create the attitude that work is a punishment.

Make Children Successful

The goal is to make your children successful so they will be successful in their adult lives. See the chores from their perspective. Look for ways to help them do chores more effectively. Show them how you complete a chore, but allow them (especially older children) to try the chore their way to see if it works better for them. Different personalities work best in different ways. As long as a child does the chore in a reasonable amount of time and with excellence, it doesn't matter how he or she does it. You may even learn a better way to do something, if you have a motivated and organized child!

Give them each, as is age appropriate, their own cleaning caddy filled with the necessary tools for their particular jobs. You can fill spray bottles partially full of cleaner or buy small sizes of products to lighten the load in the caddy. With very young children, or where chemical sensitivity is a concern, use a homemade cleaner such as vinegar-and-water solution. Buy several inexpensive one-step stools so there are no arguments about who gets to use the stool first. Put individual laundry hampers in the rooms where the children most often undress, increasing the likelihood that clothes end up in the hamper rather than on the floor. You might buy different colored laundry baskets for each child so you know who has brought clothes to the laundry room on washday or who has not put their folded clothes away.

Dad can lower closet bars, making it easier for children to hang up their clothes, and he can build accessible shelves so they can more easily put their toys away. Make sure that dresser drawers pull out easily without sticking and are low enough for a child to reach. In other words, look at your home and your expectations through a child's eyes.

Encourage

A messy child doesn't need condemnation—he needs help and encouragement. Your cheerful attitude about keeping your home is infectious. Praise your children and tell them you appreciate them as part of the family. What they do doesn't have to be perfect to earn kudos. Improvement from one time to the next is a good opportunity to give a "job well done" accolade.

Praise not only their job performance but also their character: "You showed great patience to complete that job." "You were very diligent to keep going until you finished." "You worked hard to do your job with excellence." Character is what you are building; therefore, children need to see that their choices produce particular traits in their lives.

If they do something wrong, show them again. Teaching is by precept upon precept. Hold them accountable for the things you know they can do, but encourage and cheer them on while they learn.

Training children is the hardest thing I have every done, and I didn't do it perfectly. Neither will you. Learn from your mistakes and don't give up. Your children's futures depend on your LIFE curriculum.

Marilyn Rockett is a "graduated" homeschool mom of four grown sons and Mimi to six homeschooled grandchildren. The Rocketts home taught for fifteen years before they ran out of sons to teach. Marilyn's new book, Homeschooling at the Speed of Life, *provides encouragement and organizational helps such as the Clean Room Chart. Receive a FREE download of this chart at Marilyn's web site:*

www.MarilynRockett.com

30
Reading Aloud

By Jean Hall

Read-alouds. Reading aloud. It's been the mainstay of our home school since we got off the textbook freeway and onto the scenic route. It was not a conscious choice , more like a "wrong turn" that turned into the right route. Someone introduced us to an excellent booklist, and my husband began reading aloud, a chapter a day before bedtime. This quickly became a cherished family ritual, a cozy domestic scene—Mom with her crochet, Dad in his easy chair, Daughter perched beside him, taking in every word.

We still talk about the first time we deviated from the chapter-a-day limit. We were reading *Pollyanna* and though we'd all seen the cute children's movie, the book wound us up into such a fever of anticipation that when Daughter begged for "just one more," Mom chimed in with the same plea, and Dad actually nodded and read on! . . . and on, and on, as the "just one more" became *eleven* chapters. We finished the book very late that night, an hour short of midnight, with a satisfied sigh all around. The next day, with the next book on the list, we were back to a chapter-a-day. How it built the suspense and delight, and how we all looked forward to the reading!

Textbooks

However, we were still stumbling through the textbooks during the day—our dutiful noses to the proverbial grindstone. There was little delight in our daylight studies, I'm sorry to say. Although the textbook manufacturers attempt to make the fare palatable by adding color and stories that would interest children, the sheer grind of having to get through a certain amount of material—with a struggling learner at that—was numbing. Unfortunately, I didn't know enough at the time to ask myself, "Why are we trying to do the same thing as the system that failed our daughter in the first place?"

Then something life-changing happened. We got the joyful news that our eleven-year-old would no longer be an only child. A difficult pregnancy followed. I spent most of the time on the couch. School was reduced to taking turns reading aloud to each other, and working a few math problems. I remember our daughter having to wake me up several times a day as she was reading to me.

Testing

We had mandatory annual standardized testing in our state and I worried about it. We'd abandoned the textbooks about halfway through the year, and picked up what I'd later learn were *living books*—books written by people who are knowledgeable and passionate about a subject. The authors of "living books" wish to share their excitement, and kindle interest in the reader. Such authors don't talk down to the reader, but come alongside, engaging in a conversation-of-sorts and encouraging further investigation.

For science, we read Christian Liberty's Nature Readers. For literature and history, it was the Little House books, and others. I can't remember all the titles. I wish I'd kept a list!

Testing came at the same time as the baby's arrival, and our firstborn's test scores went up! I thought, "It must be a fluke." We went back onto the textbook highway for the next year, and then another difficult pregnancy came, another struggle, physically and mentally, and the "falling back" to reading aloud. Once again, our daughter's test scores didn't suffer, but I decided not to take any chances. Back to "safe" schooling and textbooks once more. But, with a toddler and a new baby, I had a new worry. How was I going to manage juggling three grades worth of textbooks a few years hence?

At this point, I'd begun to hear about Charlotte Mason's techniques. Long before I had comprehended her six-book series and her philosophy of education, I began to try a few of the practices she'd advocated. I found out that those read-aloud books we had enjoyed so well were "living books." Now we added narration.

Narration

It was hard, with our struggling fourteen-year-old learner. I still remember that our first attempt at narration was while reading aloud from *Carry On, Mr. Bowditch*. The story was interesting, but the material so challenging that our daughter lost her way and was overwhelmed, unless I stopped every five minutes and let her narrate. In this manner, we made our way through the book.

Six weeks later, I was checking an essay assignment and was stunned. Our daughter's writing had a new spark! Not only did it exhibit imagination and power, but she was using adjectives and adverbs, and using them well! The only change in our approach had been narration. We were on to something.

I continued to learn more about narration and copywork, as well as keeping a timeline. When seeking out more booklists of living books, I stumbled across a group of like-minded parents on the Internet. We then began to read *The Burgess Bird Book* for science, narrating as we went from Hillyer's *Child's History of the World* for our history, and *A Child's Geography of the World* which I had picked up cheaply at an antique store out of curiosity a few years earlier, having heard that Hillyer books were hard to find.

Our middle daughter began narrating, of her own volition, at about age three or four. Her younger sister followed at about the same age. I didn't require narrations from them, because the advice I'd read said to require narrations starting at age six. But they narrated all the same; and just because it wasn't required until age six didn't mean I was going to squelch it before then!

Life Learning

We still read aloud. Even though our oldest daughter is in her twenties, she joins us when she can. We begin our school day by reading aloud from the Bible, each of us taking a chapter. I still find it interesting that our youngest, who struggles with reading, finds the King James Version the easiest of her day's reading, even with such long words as "transgression," "destruction," "establish" and "righteousness."

Though our two older daughters have some independent reading

as a part of their schoolwork, which they narrate orally or in writing, we still join together for some of our subjects. History and literature are popular, as are character-building stories. Dad still reads aloud in the evenings, sometimes a "fun" book and sometimes a selection from our school reading list. (At the moment he's reading *Children of the New Forest,* about the struggle between the Royalists and Cromwell's Roundheads, and very exciting it is, too, even as we are learning about everyday life of people several hundred years ago.)

Reading Expressively

There's a trick to reading aloud, however, a way to make books come to life. Even a living book can be killed if you read it in a monotone.

If you're new to reading aloud, or a little bit self-conscious, then here's your chance to shine. Even better, you'll be modeling reading with expression to your children, which they'll pick up almost unconsciously from exposure. This will build a foundation for future speaking, whether forensics, debate or oral reports.

But where do you start?

- If you didn't grow up with a good read-aloud model, you might start by listening to a great storyteller, like Jim Weiss. We checked out his tapes and CDs from the library, and enjoyed them so much that we've purchased a few for our home library. Take a simple children's story and read it aloud. Use a tape recorder, if you have trouble hearing yourself. Listen to the playback as if you're listening to a stranger; don't let self-consciousness get in your way.

- As a part of your practice, take a copy of a well-loved tale that you can write on and mark up. Use colored markers or highlighters to indicate a change of speaker. Cross out objectionable terms, if any, or write substitutions in. Give each character a distinctive voice, whether high and squeaky, or low and husky. (We usually use "normal, everyday" voice for the narrator and try for variety on the part of characters.) Practice a little, especially on stories that encourage vocal variety. *Goldilocks and the Three Bears* is a great starter story, or *Little Red Riding Hood* or *The Three Little Pigs*. Pretty soon, if you accidentally use a high, squeaky voice for the Big, Bad Wolf, you'll catch yourself and automatically change to a low growl.

- With enough practice, you'll be able to give expression to your reading even if you haven't prepared the material ahead of time. You won't need markings to remind you to change character. (Although sometimes, I do affect the wrong voice when reading, if at first it's not clear who's talking. It's the source of great amusement to my listeners when the speaker becomes apparent. It's no problem to go back and say the line again, using the proper voice, and it's an unconscious reminder of the power of vocal variety in reading.)

- Take deep breaths from the diaphragm, as if you're about to sing opera. Yes, reading aloud is performance art!

- Learn to vary your reading rate and volume. When the action is fast and furious, speed up your reading; rush through, breathless, until the action slows or stops, and find yourself literally panting for breath (along with your characters, and your audience!) at the end. If the action is slow and lazy, spread out your words, and read in a slow and lazy tone. Put in a yawn when a character is sleepy. (Caution: Yawns are contagious!) Put in a cough or two, or a realistic sneeze, when a character is ill.

It has been such a joy to hear our children reading aloud with expression, from their earliest ages, unconsciously following their parents' example.

The more life and expression you can add to your story, the more memorable. No, the purpose is not to reduce education to mere entertainment. Remember, you're starting with excellent material, and merely enhancing it. At the same time, you're celebrating the range and power of the human voice, as God designed it to be.

Jean Hall is a homeschooling mom of three, and also an author, editor, and composer. You can find examples of her music, aimed at teaching the tenets of the Christian faith, at:

www.singingthecatechism.com

Currys' Read–Aloud List

Even though Jean did not keep a list of books they read aloud, I did—at least for a few years. These are some of the titles we read aloud between 1989 and 1995. During these years, the Curry children were ages two to thirteen.

- *Tom Sawyer*
- *The Bronze Bow*
- *The Dangerous Journey*
- *Miracles on Maple Hill*
- *Swiss Family Robinson*
- *Hans Brinker* or *the Silver Skates*
- *Johnny Tremain*
- *Rebecca*
- *Farmer Boy*
- *Little House on the Prairie*
- *On the Banks of Plum Creek*
- *The Long Winter*
- *Little House in the Big Woods*
- *Little Town on the Prairie*
- *These Happy Golden Years*
- *On the Way Home*
- *Caddie Woodlawn*
- *Big Red*
- *Treasures of the Snow*
- *Door in the Wall*
- *The Black Arrow*
- *Elsie Dinsmore*

Afterword

H ow appropriate that our last chapter is on "reading aloud," the most important homeschooling activity for all ages, especially for the early grades. Read aloud from the great works suggested herein, then add variety and skills by using some of the unique ideas presented in the subject chapters; however, never let go of your focus on literature, for "the literature which children appreciate and love is the key to their soul life." (McMurry) The literary masters will then, undoubtably, have a strong moral influence upon your children.

To multiply results, simply allow the beauty of great literature to influence *you,* as you read along with your children. Perhaps more than the direct effect of these wonderful words, is your own emotion, evident when these masterpieces are read. Let them minister to your own soul first. When they are precious to you, your children will sense the immense importance of the ideas behind the works. Become one with the heart and soul, the living breathing men and women of history. Let them lift you into great ideals and fire your heart, and your children will surely follow in devotion and sacrifice; patriotism and honor.

The study of the best literature will do all these things and more, including bringing you into close companionship with your children. This is another reason why, if he is willing, the father should also be reading aloud regularly to his family.

Literature reveals the uniqueness of man, our various personalities, bringing acceptance and love for mankind and, ultimately, peace. Literature empowers. We tell ourselves, "If they could face great challenges and overcome, so can we!" Literature stimulates the brain, bringing forth intensity of thought as comparisons and judgements are made. Literature brings sweet relief from the pressures of our modern world. Literature also entertains in a way other "entertainments" can never do. It does not leave us feeling empty, but fulfills our need for joy and encouragement.

Choosing Literature by Grade Level

Even though, in this book, we have presented specific literature for each grade, as most appropriate for that grade, each title may generally be used for several grades. Hawthorne's *Wonder Book,* for instance, could be used in any grade from the third through the eighth. The question is, however, "What grade level is it *best* suited to?" Although older students may get some enjoyment out of *Wonder Book,* younger children may not understand it completely; thus, it is most suited to the spiritual and developmental thought level of children at about fourth or fifth grade.

In choosing literature for each grade, first look at the material and secondly the language and vocabulary. The material is of primary importance, even if we must "force" the children into the level of the language of the book, thus beneficially bringing upon them early growth in language skills. Nevertheless, we may later find that for our particular children, a book just needs to be put aside for a year or two. This is quite acceptable. As I have stated in my other books, you are the creator of your own homeschool, and should adapt your curriculum to your own family and their interests.

Teacher preparation? Get out of the classroom. Go forth into the meadows, groves and streams in the company of Bryant, Longfellow and Whittier. Read a page from *Fields with God.* Take a draught of Creation's waters, and allow them to sustain, nourish and calm you, preparing you for the time of your life, in sharing great literature with your children—the most natural and blessed learning activity ever.

Nature Literature

oets have written extensively on the beauty, majesty and wonder of nature. They lift our hearts to the Creator in joy and thankfulness for his mercy and love. Even patriotism is encouraged by the natural beauty of our homeland.

Regarding curriculum, literature of the natural world teaches not only awe, but facts. It inspires to greater curiosity and resulting knowledge. It may not be pure science, but it is a powerful partner to this field of study.

Here is a sampling of American poets and authors to get you started. There are many more appropriate works available, by these authors, and others. (I have written a nature devotional, *Fields with God,* especially for mothers, particularly homeschooling mothers.)

Nature Study

William Cullen Bryant
- "The Forest Hymn"
- "The Death of the Flowers"
- "The Return of the Birds"
- "A Summer Ramble"
- "The Fringed Gentian"
- "The Hunter of the Prairies"
- "The White-footed Deer"
- "To a Waterfowl"
- "Thanatopsis"

Henry Wadsworth Longfellow
- "Hiawatha"
- "Evangeline"

John Greenleaf Whittier
- "Barefoot Boy"
- "Songs of Labor"
- "Among the Hills"
- "Snow Bound"

Nathaniel Hawthorne
- "Tales of the White Hills"

Oliver Wendell Holmes
- "Spring"

James Russell Lowell
- "Indian Summer Reverie"
- "The Oak"

Science

John Burroughs
- "Wake Robin"
- "Birds and Bees"
- "Sharp Eyes"

Henry David Thoreau
- "Succession of Forest Trees"
- "Wild Apples"

Charles Dudley Warner
- "A Hunting of the Deer"

Index

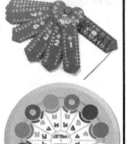

220

OUR YOUNG FOLKS' JOSEPHUS
ANTIQUITIES OF THE JEWS AND THE JEWISH WARS

"Jump back in time to a place where historical accounts of the Hebrews are brought to life in an exciting narrative style. The history of Ancient Israel is revealed in a first-hand account from the great historian Flavius Josephus. OUR YOUNG FOLKS' JOSEPHUS is a compilation of his two greatest works, ANTIQUITIES OF THE JEWS and THE JEWISH WARS. You'll marvel at the history that is played-out before your eyes. A journey that begins with the call of Abraham and ends with the destruction of Jerusalem and the fall of Massada...this is a must-have for any bookshelf." ~Eclectic Homeschool Online

This work is an invaluable supplement to the study of ancient Israel, covering a broad period of time in detail, yet at a pace suitable for the upper elementary and middleschool student. Beautifully illustrated with antique lithographic art.

PaideaClassics.Org

Also available at Amazon.com (Marketplace), Rainbow Resource, The Book Peddler, TanglewoodEducation.com, Arx Publishing and other fine homeschool retailers.

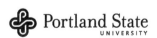

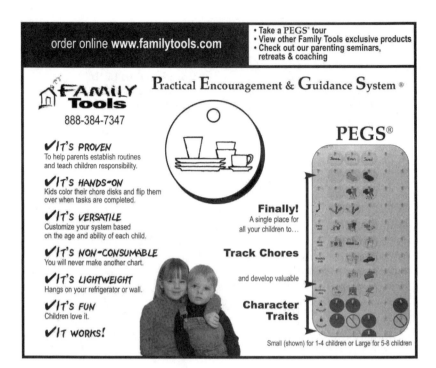

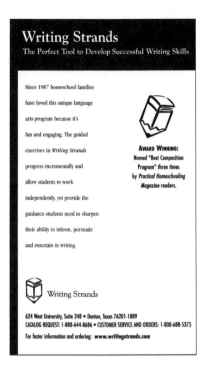

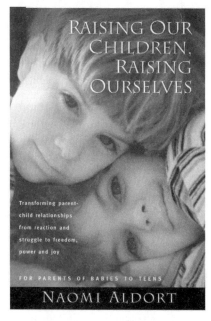

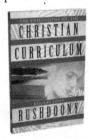

Summit Ministries

Summit uses a variety of conferences to train Christians to analyze alternative worldviews and equip them to champion the Christian faith.

Summer Conferences

Intensive two-week educational conferences (for high school and college students) that analyze the major humanistic worldviews of our day, contrasting them with the Christian worldview.

Spring Conferences

Aggressive one-week educational conferences (for pastors, educators and adults) that analyzes the major humanistic worldviews of our day, contrasting them with the Christian worldview.

Worldview Weekends

Concentrated weekend educational conferences (for pastors, educators, adults and young people) that analyze the major issues of our day, addressing them from the Christian worldview.

Understanding the Times is a 90 or 180-day worldview and Bible curriculum for 12th grade. Through this class, students will learn how to analyze and disarm the competing worldviews of our day and to defend the Christian worldview.

Lightbearers is a 90 or 180-day worldview and Bible curriculum for 8th grade. Through this class, students will learn the Christian worldview and how that worldview relates to theology, philosophy, ethics, biology, economics, etc.

Building on the Rock is a 6-year worldview and Bible curriculum for 1st - 6th grade. Through these classes, students will not only learn the Bible, but they will see that the Bible is true and applicale to every area of their lives.

Worldviews in Focus is a 13-week Sunday School curriculum that addresses the various ideas shaping our current culture from a Christian worldivew

www.summit.org

232

"WHY NOT DRINK?"

1. EVERY YEAR IN THE USA ALCOHOL KILLS MORE YOUNG PEOPLE THAN ALL OTHER ILLICIT DRUGS COMBINED. HOW MANY YOUNG PEOPLE ARE KILLED EVERY YEAR BY ALCOHOL?

   A. 3,000+   B. 5,000+   C. 7,000+

2. Alcohol Poisoning or AOD (alcohol overdose) claims about 4,000 lives every year and most are preteens, teenagers, and college-age young people.

   A. False   B. True

3. Alcohol is implicated in what percentage of all college academic problems?

   A. 10%   B. 25%   C. 40%

4. What is the approximate annual carnage of death and injury recorded in police reports where drinking in moderation and driving is the cause?

   A. 18,000   B. 22,000   C. 26,000

Dear Parents, These questions reveal the **GREAT DANGER** alcohol poses. We have a God-given responsiblity to warn those God has put in our care. Remember these numbers represent real young people like those you know and love. In the USA, alcohol will claim the lives of 70,000 young people over the next 10 years. Find out how to combat this threat in "Why Not Drink? Nine points that support total abstinence from alcohol" by Gary G. Ashe. This book is only $8.99. Call **800-421-8906** or visit Valley Book and Bible Store online at **www.vbb.com** and click on Exclusive Titles. FREE teaching posters are included.

Christian Education Author, Gary G. Ashe

Answers: 1.C 2.B 3.C 4.C

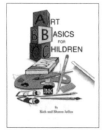  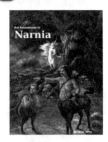

Great resources from WISDOM'S GATE Publishing...

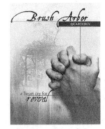